KASPAROV

THE HISTORIC CHESS MATCH BETWEEN MAN AND MACHINE

AND DEEP BLUE

Bruce Pandolfini

A FIRESIDE BOOK
Published by Simon & Schuster

FIRESIDE
Rockefeller Center
1230 Avenue of the Americas
New York, NY 10020

FIRESIDE and colophon are registered trademarks
of Simon & Schuster Inc.

Designed by Stanley S. Drate/Folio Graphics Co. Inc.

Manufactured in the United States of America

10   9   8   7   6   5   4   3   2   1

Library of Congress Cataloging-in-Publication Data

Pandolfini, Bruce.
    Kasparov and Deep Blue : the historic chess match between man and
machine / Bruce Pandolfini.
        p.   cm.
        "A Fireside book."
        1. Kasparov, G. K. (Garri Kimovich)   2. Deep Blue (Computer)
    3. Chess—Tournaments—Pennsylvania—Philadelphia.   4. Chess—
    Collections of games.   I. Title.
    GV1438.K38P34   1997
    794.1'59—dc21   97-30448
                                                              CIP

ISBN 0-684-84852-X

CONTENTS

INTRODUCTION   7

HOW TO READ CHESS MOVES IN ALGEBRAIC
NOTATION   9

GAME 1   13

GAME 2   40

GAME 3   67

GAME 4   93

GAME 5   118

GAME 6   142

AFTERWORD   161

THE GAMES OF MATCH ONE   163

SOURCES   171

INTRODUCTION

On February 17, 1996, in Philadelphia, the City of Brotherly Love, Garry Kasparov rose from a chess table full of triumph and glory. He had just vanquished IBM's Deep Blue supercomputer in the sixth and final game of a head-to-head battle that was depicted as the ultimate test of man vs. machine.

The humans had won by a score of 4–2, but it wasn't even that close. Kasparov, perhaps the greatest chess champion of all time, had demonstrated a command of strategy far beyond the machine's crunching brute-force tactics. Deep Blue could assess 100 million positions per second, but it lacked the sensitivity needed to grasp the subtlety of position play, the hallmark of true mastery.

Cut to the Big Apple, May 11, 1997, and we have a very different scene. Picture an embattled warrior, the weight of humanity on his shoulders, rising from a chessboard in anger and despair, walking off the stage in total defeat.

By a score of 3.5–2.5, the new and improved Deep Blue had outlasted and finally conquered its brilliant human rival in the rematch of the century, winning the last game so decisively that pundits were saying the result had to be fixed, that Kasparov threw the last game to create maximum interest in Kasparov vs. Deep Blue III.

That idea was squelched within days, when IBM, with its stock soaring, and perhaps miffed at what the company deemed to be the champion's rude and insulting behavior, announced at a press conference in New York that it had no intention of giving him another match.

No, IBM had made its profit, and its point. A supercomputer, developed and fine-tuned by ingenious programmers, technicians, and grandmasters, with the megabacking of a giant, multi-national corporation, could indeed compete with the best chess brain in the world.

Why this turnabout happened, how it affects the game of chess, and the broader question, what it means to the future of humanity, are some of the issues that prompted me to write this book.

I also sensed that by attempting to come to grips with these issues, it would be possible to analyze the play-by-play action of this historic encounter in a manner helpful to a wide audience. I thought the match itself, especially because of the clash in styles between Kasparov's intuitive, more discriminating approach and Deep Blue's no-nonsense reliance on raw calculation, would provide an excellent vehicle to elucidate the principles of chess and how moves are determined.

The result is this volume, which explains the moves of the match while clarifying numerous chess paradigms and their applications. Along the way, I've tried to reveal some of the game's art and beauty, its practical value, and how much fun it is to play.

HOW TO READ CHESS MOVES IN ALGEBRAIC NOTATION

To understand algebraic notation you must view the chessboard as an eight-by-eight grid. Every square on the grid has its own name, based on the intersecting file and rank.

Files, the rows of squares going up and down, are lettered **a** through **h.** Ranks, the rows of squares going across, are numbered **1** through **8.**

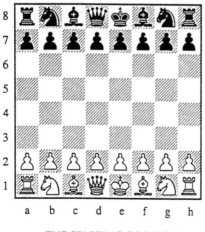

THE STARTING POSITION

Squares are designated by combining those letters and numbers. For each name, the letter is lowercase and appears first, before the number. Thus, in the diagram of the starting position, White's queen occupies **d1** and Black's **d8.**

There is only one perspective in the algebraic system: White's. All squares are named from White's side of the board. For example, the a-file is always on White's left and Black's right. The first rank is always the one closest to White and farthest from Black.

The algebraic grid below gives the names and positions of all the squares. You might find it helpful to photocopy it and use it as a bookmark so it's always there as a reminder.

BLACK

a8	b8	c8	d8	e8	f8	g8	h8
a7	b7	c7	d7	e7	f7	g7	h7
a6	b6	c6	d6	e6	f6	g6	h6
a5	b5	c5	d5	e5	f5	g5	h5
a4	b4	c4	d4	e4	f4	g4	h4
a3	b3	c3	d3	e3	f3	g3	h3
a2	b2	c2	d2	e2	f2	g2	h2
a1	b1	c1	d1	e1	f1	g1	h1

WHITE

THE ALGEBRAIC GRID. EVERY SQUARE HAS A UNIQUE NAME.

Other Symbols

You should also familiarize yourself with the following symbols:

Symbol	Meaning
K	king
Q	queen
R	rook
B	bishop
N	knight

P	pawn (not used in algebraic notation)
–	moves to
×	captures
+	check
#	checkmate
0–0	castles kingside
0–0–0	castles queenside
!	good move
?	bad move
!!	brilliant move
??	blunder
!?	probably a good move
?!	probably a bad move
e.p.	en passant
1–0	White wins
0–1	Black wins

Note that though **P** stands for pawn, it is not used in algebraic notation (though it is used in descriptive notation, which is not necessary for this book). If no indication of the moving unit is given in algebraic notation, the move is a pawn move.

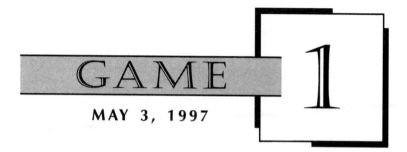

GAME 1

MAY 3, 1997

WHITE: **Garry Kasparov**

BLACK: **Deep Blue**

OPENING: **Reti Opening/King's Indian Attack**

ECO CODE: **A07**

RESULT: **Kasparov wins in 45 moves**

SCORE: **Kasparov 1—Deep Blue 0**

THE MOVES

NO.	WHITE	BLACK	NO.	WHITE	BLACK
1.	Nf3	d5	24.	f3	Nxe3
2.	g3	Bg4	25.	Nxe3	Be7
3.	b3	Nd7	26.	Kh1	Bg5
4.	Bb2	e6	27.	Re2	a4
5.	Bg2	Ngf6	28.	b4	f5
6.	0-0	c6	29.	exf5	e4
7.	d3	Bd6	30.	f4	Bxe2
8.	Nbd2	0-0	31.	fxg5	Ne5
9.	h3	Bh5	32.	g6	Bf3
10.	e3	h6	33.	Bc3	Qb5
11.	Qe1	Qa5	34.	Qf1	Qxf1 +
12.	a3	Bc7	35.	Rxf1	h5
13.	Nh4	g5	36.	Kg1	Kf8
14.	Nhf3	e5	37.	Bh3	b5
15.	e4	Rfe8	38.	Kf2	Kg7
16.	Nh2	Qb6	39.	g4	Kh6
17.	Qc1	a5	40.	Rg1	hxg4
18.	Re1	Bd6	41.	Bxg4	Bxg4
19.	Ndf1	dxe4	42.	Nxg4 +	Nxg4 +
20.	dxe4	Bc5	43.	Rxg4	Rd5
21.	Ne3	Rad8	44.	f6	Rd1
22.	Nhf1	g4	45.	g7	Black resigns
23.	hxg4	Nxg4		(1–0)	

MAN BITES MACHINE

The first game of IBM's Kasparov vs. Deep Blue rematch started, and finished, with surprise. With the White pieces, the world champion began somewhat reservedly, playing a quiet variation of the King's Indian Attack. Kasparov didn't move a soldier beyond his own third rank until the thirteenth move, and neither player captured anything until Deep Blue broke the peace on move nineteen, fixing the central war zone by exchanging king-pawns.

Kasparov's tentative approach seemed to confuse the computer, which proceeded to waste time, moving pieces helter-skelter, without direction or concert. In particular, two tempi were lost repositioning Black's queen and dark-square bishop.

Eventually, White's apparent taciturnity provoked Deep Blue into several risky pawn escapades, trying to force its steely mind on the champ. But Kasparov defended with great sangfroid, and by a series of accurate counterattacking strokes, including the valiant sacrifice of a rook for a bishop, refuted Deep Blue's unsound aggression.

Once queens were traded, Black's endgame looked like Swiss cheese, chewy and replete with holes. It didn't take long before White convoyed a pair of monstrous connective pawns up the kingside, issuing deadly threats in their paths. With no way to stop White from promoting both pawns to new queens, Deep Blue gave up on its 45th move. The wonder was that Kasparov had beaten Deep Blue in the area of its greatest strength. The human had outcalculated the machine.

White	Black
Garry Kasparov	Deep Blue

1.   Nf3   . . .

White's first move signals the Reti Opening, named after the Czech-Hungarian grandmaster Richard Reti (1889–1929), one of the founders of modern chess.

The classic approach to opening play is to occupy the central squares with pieces and pawns right from the beginning. Reti advocated a different approach: first fight for the center from the wing, and only after insuring control of the middle region, occupy it with pieces and pawns. The key weapons in this strategy are bishop-pawns and flanked bishops.

1.   . . .   d5

This thrust, actually occupying the center with a pawn, is contrary to Reti's method. White could now try to mount pressure against d5. One way is with the c-pawn, moving it to c4. Kasparov eschews this, but employs a supportive idea, soon flanking the king-bishop at g2. This type of development is called a fianchetto.

2.   g3   . . .

Starting the fianchetto of the light-square bishop.

2.   . . .   Bg4

Activating the queen-bishop with the possibility of taking the f3-knight, doubling White's pawns. Generally, doubled pawns (two pawns of the same color on the same file) are a liability. They can no longer defend each other, and the front one hampers the back one's forward movement.

But sometimes when you accept a weakness you get compensation. If Black here were to inflict doubled pawns on White by capturing on f3, it would have to surrender a bishop for a knight. Though bishops and knights are approximately equal in value, each worth about three pawns, most positions favor bishops.

To exchange a bishop for a knight so early, before the right battle plan crystallizes, implies a concession, even though the other side ends up with doubled pawns. Since it's not clear who gets the better deal, Kasparov rightly ignores Deep Blue's "threat."

3.   b3   . . .

Beginning a second fianchetto before completing the first. As a rule, one should finish what one starts, or nothing gets done. But world-champion Kasparov has every intention of fulfilling his tasks. He's just hoping to lead the computer astray by introducing an unusual move order. Who knows what pitfalls await Deep Blue if from the very start it is obliged to think for itself, unable to draw on its voluminous opening book of programmed moves?

3.   . . .   Nd7

In addition to developing the queen-knight, this move also begins the fight for e5. It at once prevents the counterattack, Nf3-e5, hitting the g4-bishop. But why not place the knight on the third rank, at c6, where it's more centralized?

The answer is that developing the knight to c6 impedes the movement of Black's c-pawn. Black needs the option of moving the c-pawn in order to attack White's center, to support its own d-pawn. Also it needs to clear a path for the queen to the queenside along the a5-d8 diagonal.

It's surprising that Deep Blue didn't take the knight, Bg4xf3. Such an exchange of bishop for knight is more committal than developing the queen-knight, but it infects White with doubled pawns, a real turn-on for most chessic machines.

4.   Bb2   . . .

White completes the queenside fianchetto and adds a second guard to e5, thwarting the thrust e7-e5. Black could still enforce this push by first exchanging bishop for knight on f3 and then advancing the king-pawn, though there's a Catch-22.

Computers delight in plaguing their opponents with doubled pawns, but they also love bishops. To inflict the doubled pawns, the blue menace would have to part with a bishop, an object it doesn't cede lightly. Thus we have conflicting principles, which some computers could blow a fuse over. Here, Deep Blue opts to retain its beloved bishop, and its sanity.

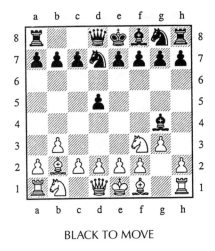

BLACK TO MOVE

4.   . . .   e6

Black renounces the intention of a two-square king-pawn advance for now, while bolstering the d-pawn and releasing the dark-square bishop.

5.   Bg2   Ngf6

6.   0-0   . . .

Having castled, White is now ready to begin operations in the center. As a general rule, it's a no-no to engage in central activity with your king still in the middle, for as avenues of attack open, your king becomes prey to the opponent's falcons. In addition to safeguarding the king, castling also brings a rook closer to the active zone, where it can festively participate.

6.   . . .   c6

This cautious push fortifies the d-pawn, creating a central phalanx of pawns at c6, d5, and e6. Such a formation is referred to as a strong-point defense because the head pawn, d5, is protected by two other pawns. The advance also unblocks the a5-d8 diagonal for the queen. A further point is that with d5 additionally guarded by the c-pawn, Black is free to pursue the earlier scheme of advancing the e-pawn. This is typical. Often a good plan is set aside until the time is propitious.

7.   d3   ...

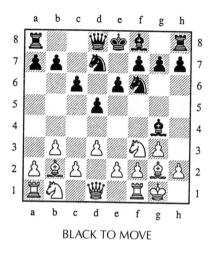

BLACK TO MOVE

Kasparov clears d2 for the queen-knight, which also prepares an eventual assault against the center by moving the king-pawn to e4. The champion is playing rather carefully, with none of his forces extended beyond the third rank. Having never seen a game by the new and improved Deep Blue, Garry proceeds with circumspection, hoping to get a better read.

7.   ...   Bd6

The machine played this natural move instantly, meaning either of two things: the position reflects the myriad contingencies in its book knowledge, or, more likely, Deep Blue had already analyzed the situation on Kasparov's previous turn, while Garry was thinking.

The point of Bf8-d6 is at least twofold. It engages the dark-square bishop actively, while clearing the home rank for castling; and it lays further claim to e5, with the idea of advancing the king-pawn.

But there's a potential shortcoming. With the bishop on d6, White might have the opportunity later on to fork the bishop and f6-knight by advancing his e-pawn to e5. (A fork is an attack issued by a friendly unit to two or more enemy units on the same turn.) Of course, the computer would not overlook such tactical dastardliness, nor would the computer's opponent.

8.   Nbd2   ...

White follows up on his blueprint, positioning the queen-knight so as not to obstruct the b2-bishop's long diagonal.

> *A principle of development is to station the pieces harmoniously, with support, and without stepping on each other's toes. Too often, newcomers develop mindlessly, without rhyme or reason, and their forces wind up clashing and crashing into each other.*
>
> *How do you avoid incongruent development? Sometimes it can't be helped, but you can strive for harmony by attempting to anticipate problems and by working with a plan. Try not to develop any piece without considering the placement of all the others as well.*

8.   ...   0-0

And now Black has also castled. Both players are ready for business. Once you have actuated your minor pieces (bishops and knights) and gotten your king to safety, the final phase of initial development is "connecting the rooks." From the start, this usually takes between 10–12 moves and is ordinarily realized by moving the queen off the home rank so that the rooks actually defend each other.

After the players have connected their rooks, the game assumes a transitional stage between opening and middlegame. We could almost say that the chief objective of the first dozen moves is to obtain a favorable middlegame, with optimal chances to accumulate positional advantages. Once these advantages become concrete, tangible, and especially material, the next step is to simplify to a winning endgame. That's how it's done on paper.

The key is dominance. You have superiority if you can control the flow of play and direct the game's ultimate course.

9.   h3   ...

Forcing Black to decide. Is it going to take the knight or retreat? Knowing the proclivity of Deep Blue to retain bishops, the answer can be surmised.

9.	. . .	Bh5
10.	e3	. . .

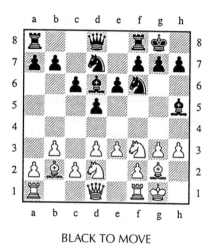

BLACK TO MOVE

This brings us to one of those what-if junctures. What would have happened if White had traded a knight for a bishop with 10. g4 Bg6 11. Nh4? Would Black have sacrificed a knight for the attack by 11. . . . Nf6xg4?

Obviously, 12. hxg4 walks into 12. . . . Qxh4, with White's king in real trouble. So the champion would first have to take the bishop, 12. Nxg6. After 12. . . . fxg6 (to open the f-file for Black's rook) 13. hxg4, White is ahead, a piece for a pawn. But then Black has the invasionary counter 13. . . . Qh4, and suddenly White's king is menaced. Note that 14. Nf3 is met by 14. . . . Rxf3!, when White can't retake on f3 because of the mate threat at h2.

Kasparov's move, 10. e3, solves these problems, whether White intends subsequently to enter upon this variation or not. With the king-pawn moved to e3, White's queen defends g4 and can capture on that square in the above analysis, which would refute Black's unsound sacrifice on g4.

10.	. . .	h6

Deep Blue is still trying to find ways to preserve the light-square bishop (and to avoid the doubled pawns that would ensue from an eventual Nh4xg6). This explains the weakening pawn move, h7-h6. Now the meandrous bishop has a safe haven at h7, but Black's kingside has been compromised. Let's see if retaining the bishop is worth the trouble.

11.   Qe1   . . .

By sidling the queen to e1, Kasparov breaks the pin on his f3-knight, which is no longer shielding the queen from the h5-bishop. The queen also supports the possible advance of the king-pawn to e4. On the downside, White's home rank stays blocked, with the rooks remaining unconnected. White might have instead played his queen to e2, but that wouldn't have ended the pin on f3.

Chess is a game of decisions and choices. Most of the time, you can't get everything you want. To achieve reasonable gains you generally have to make sensible concessions. Here, with his insight and strategic mastery, the world champion has the edge on his rival.

11.   . . .   Qa5?

Not the best place for the queen. It's sensible to connect the rooks, but the queen serves better at either c7 or e7, both of which clear the back rank and reinforce the king-pawn's advance to e5. If there's a tactical point to Qd8-a5, it's to threaten Bd6-a3, trading bishops and trying to capitalize on the weakened queenside dark squares.

12.   a3   . . .

Nullifying Black's intended intrusion on a3 and arming White with the ability to push the b-pawn. Black would then have to waste time moving the queen to safety.

12.   . . .   Bc7?

Now this is a strange, computerlike move that few grandmasters would consider. Was Deep Blue afraid of an impending fork at e5? Was it merely envisioning a redeployment to b6 and the a7-g1 diagonal, pinning the f2-pawn? Or did it determine a need to protect the queen from White's queen, concerned with a possible discovery along the a5-e1 diagonal? However you cut it, dropping the bishop back to c7 costs time and interferes with the queen's line of retreat. Advantage White.

13.   Nh4   . . .

White seemingly prepares to advance the g-pawn, pushing the bishop back to g6, where it can be taken by the knight. The computer loses a bishop for a knight (also called losing the minor exchange), and is constrained to accept a doubled pawn on g6, neither of which is palatable to the machine's brain.

What's all the fuss about bishops and knights if the two minor pieces are judged to be relatively equal? Aren't both worth roughly the same, three pawns each? Well, yes, and no. Although the two have approximately the same exchange value, they do different things and have diverse talents.

Bishops are long-range pieces that work best in open positions, especially from afar. Knights need to be close for efficacy, their mobility increasing with centralization. It helps if the steed is secured by friendly pawns and pieces, and if no enemy pawn can drive it away. Place a knight on the edge, however, and you'll have to pray it isn't lassoed and corralled. Bishops can dominate the center even from a corner without fear of being harassed.

True, knights are equipped to attack every square on the chessboard, whereas bishops travel on squares of one color only, half the chessboard remaining inaccessible to them. But the bishop has the ability to lose a tempo usefully by moving along the diagonal it already controls. Knights can't do this. Every time a knight moves, it guards a whole new set of squares.

Nevertheless, the ultimate decision, to prefer a knight or bishop, depends on the position at hand, and the concrete circumstances that prevail. Sure, bishops do well in open positions and knights in closed ones, though bishops tend to get the better of knights in a majority of situations.

Ideally, opt for the minor piece that works best in the given circumstances. Since early on you can't always determine where the game is headed, it makes sense to delay permanent commitments, such as exchanging a bishop for a knight unnecessarily, until the right course of action becomes clear.

Chasing the h5-bishop was hardly White's only scheme in the position. To fuel a kingside attack, he might have been thinking of advancing the f-pawn, as well as the g-pawn. A surer way to achieve this objective, however, was to pirouette the f3-knight to h2, where it couldn't be driven back by the g-pawn.

13.   ...   g5?

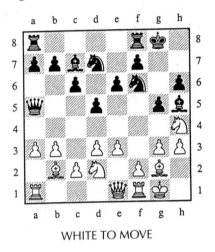

WHITE TO MOVE

For Deep Blue, things are very clear. It wants to keep the light-square bishop so much it's willing to accept the outcome of a precarious kingside pawn move. White's knight must withdraw, and the bishop survives—for now.

14.   Nhf3   e5

So Black is the first to mobilize in the middle. Note how Deep Blue's aligned center pawns assail, across the frontier line, a block of four squares, including c4, d4, e4, and f4.

It's curious. Fourteen moves have been played—that's fourteen for each side—not a single thing has been captured, and Garry Kasparov, the greatest attacking player of all time, has nothing advanced beyond the third rank. Is he running scared or being cagey?

15.   e4!   ...

Push comes to shove. White fixes Black's king-pawn in place and stops its forward procession. Kasparov also seizes control of f5, a square that could figure prominently in White's kingside campaign.

15.   ...   Rfe8

Centering a rook and reinforcing the king-pawn against a future e-file discovery, if ever such a strategem has potency. The square f8 is also made available for other pieces, such as the d7-knight.

16.   Nh2   ...

Is White contemplating the perilous sacrifice f2-f4, attempting to open the a1-h8 diagonal for his bishop and the f-file for his rook? Probably not. Perhaps he thought about disputing g4 by Bg2-f3 and Nh2-g4.

16.   ...   Qb6

Pinning the f-pawn and preparing to move the rook-pawn to a5 and then a4, striking at b3. The b3-pawn provides shelter for the b2-bishop from the linear attack of Black's queen. On the other hand, this retrenching of Black's queen to b6 confirms a loss of time in moving it originally to a5.

17.   Qc1!   ...

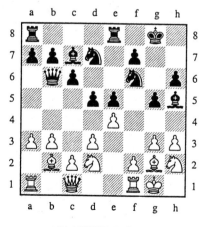

BLACK TO MOVE

A splendid transfer on the home rank. Not only does Kasparov prop his bishop, he positions his queen to take dead aim at Black's impaired kingside, with the pawns at g5 and h6 the prime targets. The shift also vacates e1 for the king-rook. And if the rook moves to e1, suddenly f1 becomes accessible to a knight. From there, a knight can reach the outpost at f5 in two moves (Nf1-e3-f5). That's maximum efficiency within confined quarters.

17.   . . .   a5

Per plan. Deep Blue stultifies b3-b4 and prepares a further advance of the a-pawn. Black's queen also gets some breathing room.

18.   Re1   Bd6

What's going on here? Which one of Deep Blue's 512 micro-processors is responsible for this? The idea seems to be to reposition the bishop to c5, doubling the pressure on the debilitated f2 (with the rook now on e1). The move also unblocks the a5-d8 diagonal for Black's queen. But the bishop's been to d6 before. Black seems to have squandered at least two tempi.

A line (rank, file, or diagonal) is considered closed when each player has a friendly obstructive pawn on the line. A player can move along the closed line only as far as his own impeding pawn. Neither player can go beyond his friendly obstacle to reach the other end of the line.

Pawn obstacles tend to persist. They are relatively immobile. You can't move them out of the way, just like that. But pieces (anything but a pawn) are something else. The minor pieces (knights and bishops), for example, usually can be relocated without much trouble, unclogging the key square or route at a moment's notice.

From this it follows that, if you want to be able to utilize a particular square or line, you should overprotect the crucial spot of potential exchange to be able to take back with pieces, not just pawns. (Actually, try to guard the menaced square with both.)

19.   Ndf1   . . .

Continuing the plan of redistributing the wealth to the king-side. White's knight is headed for the hole at f5 and the vulnerable h6-pawn.

19.   . . .   dxe4

Here we go. It's move nineteen and we have the first exchange of the game. Black releases the tension by capturing on e4. White can no longer take back with a knight, the queen-knight having just jumped from d2 to f1. White will recapture with the d-pawn, barring from White's use e4 and the e-file.

Generally, you can deny the opponent use of a line (or a square) by fixing one of his own pawns in place. This is typically done by forcing exchanges.

20.   dxe4   . . .

If White had taken back with the bishop, Bg2xe4, he would surely have encountered the capture Nf6xe4. All other things being equal, no way Deep Blue turns down the opportunity to garner a bishop for a knight.

20.   . . .   Bc5

As expected, by moving this bishop for the fourth time, Black forms a battery along the a7-g1 diagonal. Now f2 must be guarded or shielded.

21.   Ne3   . . .

The knight screens the attack on f2, while moving closer to the optimal target, f5. Moreover, from e3, the knight may also land annoyingly on c4, if tactics against f2 ever allow. Here, though, if the knight moves to f5 or c4, Black's bishop can take on f2 with check. Ouch.

21.   . . .   Rad8

Placing the other rook on a central file, an open one at that. (A file is open if no pawns block it.) Now all of Black's pieces have been activated, whereas White's queen-rook remains untouched.

22.   Nhf1   . . .

Strengthening e3, and positioning one knight to replace the other on an exchange.

22.   ...   g4?

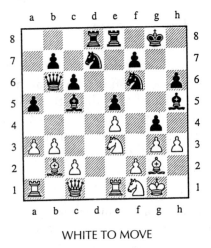

WHITE TO MOVE

This looks very wrong and illustrates a basic difference between the computer and a grandmaster. A world-class simian would never play such a risky, antipositional pawn advance without being quite sure of its correctness. If this spiking movement doesn't gain a concrete advantage, Black will be left with a ruined, exposed kingside, with White's queen and supportive pieces already poised to strike.

> *Pawn moves are permanent. You can't take them back. If they work, fine. But if they don't, you're stuck with the consequences, because pawns can't move back to where they were. When a pawn advances, it can never again guard the squares it used to guard. These abandoned squares tend to become weak because of the loss of friendly pawn protection. They must rely on the kindness of pieces.*

Black wasted several tempi, moving the bishop from d6 to c7 and back to d6. The loss of time hurts on some level, but Deep

Blue was still able to maneuver the bishop back to where it was to pursue another plan without palpable disadvantage. But, even when there's enough time, pawns can never go home again. The infernal machine must accept the effects of its errant g-pawn's last move.

23.   hxg4   Nxg4

With this recapture, Black zeroes in on f2 and e3, potential weak links along the a7-g1 diagonal. White could exchange knights on g4 and then play Nf1-e3, but then he wouldn't be able to continue as he does in the game, following with f2-f3, because of the pin on the a7-g1 diagonal.

24.   f3?   . . .

This bantam pawn move strengthens e4 while attacking the g4-knight. In general, it's a good idea not to let enemy pieces sit on squares in your half of the board, particularly near your king.

There's a snag to White's move, however; it renders the a7-g1 diagonal more susceptible. White winds up with a pinned knight on e3. Maybe Garry should have held the f-pawn back instead trading knights on g4 and then positioning the f1-knight on e3. White would clearly have the edge.

24.   . . .   Nxe3
25.   Nxe3   . . .

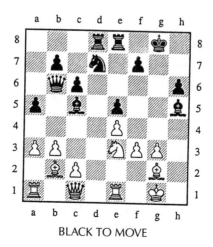

BLACK TO MOVE

Of course, Black doesn't want to swap any further. Its position has exploitable weaknesses, so it wouldn't want to simplify to a losing ending. Moreover, Deep Blue hasn't gained any material, and too many trades will dissipate the attack.

> *A pinned piece or pawn can't run away. Unless your opponent has a pin-breaking tactic, don't take his pinned unit before deriving certain advantage. As a rule, once you've pinned a piece, pile pressure on it with additional forces, trying to reduce your opponent's options, until you win material or extract valuable concessions.*

Which brings us back to the actual game. If the pressure against White's pinned knight on e3 is to be increased, how is Deep Blue going to do it?

25.   . . .   Be7!

That's how, or at least the start or it: by transferring the bishop to g5.

26.   Kh1   . . .

Capitalizing on the one-move respite to move the king out of the pin. The knight is now free to go.

26.   . . .   Bg5

It's still not safe to go in the water. Just as White finds himself free of one pin, a new one comes along and the problem persists. Once again the e3-knight is immobilized, prevented from reaching knight heaven at f5, pinned by the bishop to the queen. At g5 the bishop also plays another role: as hero/defender of the c1-h6 diagonal.

27.   Re2   . . .

This small, but precise, rook move helps assuage the pressure. Besides securing the second rank against invasion, it also provides the champion a practical way to end the pin with counterthreats. His queen can commute along the home rank toward the kingside. White's pieces are coordinating beautifully.

27.   ...   a4

Attacks the b-pawn, more or less forcing White's response.

28.   b4   f5!?

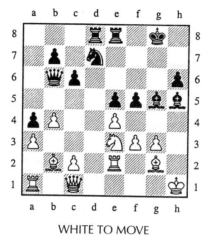

WHITE TO MOVE

Wow! A bold sacrifice, played in a flash, which means the computer predicted Kasparov's previous move and had worked out its response on the champion's time. (Kasparov played his next few replies also quite quickly.)

For the most part, this type of crazy situation—complicated, highly tactical, defiant of rules—tends to favor the computer, with its brute-force approach, being able to calculate 200 million positions per second.

But Kasparov's no analytic slouch either. Even if ciphering is the computer's domain, Garry is probably the best mortal chess calculator there is. Combine this skill with Kasparov's far greater understanding of chess, especially in his intuitive feel for position play, and suddenly Deep Blue is the underdog. Or is it?

29.   exf5   ...

Garry accepts the challenge. He takes the offered pawn, going where no human has gone before: headlong into all thirty-two nodes of Deep Blue's wonderfully mysterious and artificial brain. Since computers never surrender material lightly, it's safe to assume the sacrifice is logical. But does it work?

29. ...   e4

Black fires at the pinned f3-pawn. If White moves the f-pawn, say f3xe4, he hangs (leaves in a position to be captured for free) the rook on e2. Meanwhile, Black threatens to wreak havoc, taking on f3 with the e-pawn, forking two White pieces. How is Garry Kasparov going to wend his way through such complexity?

30.   f4!   ...

That's how. By sacrificing "the exchange." Kasparov offers the rook on e2. If Deep Blue takes it, the machine loses the dark-square bishop on g5. Deep Blue comes out ahead in material.

So who gets the better deal in the present situation? With sole regard to material, Deep Blue. But chess is all about intelligence overcoming the forces of nature, and what better proponent of mind over chess matter than Garry Kasparov?

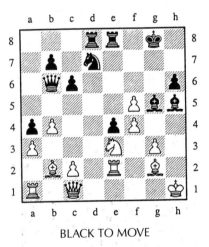

BLACK TO MOVE

30.   ...   Bxe2

Deep Blue eats the material. What did you expect? The real question is, could it have gained an extra pawn in the bargain by first taking on f4 (Bg5xf4), and after White retakes (g3xf4), then chomping the rook (Bh5xe2)?

The answer is, yes, especially if losing doesn't mean the same thing as it does to humans. In this imagined line (30. . . . Bxf4

31. gxf4 Bxe2), White has the devastating rejoinder 32. Qg1!, holding e3 and threatening a vicious discovery to Black's suddenly airy king. Moreover, from g1, White's queen has a direct route to h2 and the h-file. As you play through the possibilities over an analysis board, dear Homo sapiens, take solace. You'll find that Black's resources are bleak.

> *You win "the exchange" when you give up a minor piece (a bishop or a knight) and get for it a rook. Minor pieces are worth about three pawns each. Rooks are worth about five pawns each. So, if you lose "the exchange," you lose about two pawns in value.*
>
> *The reader must be careful, making sure not to confuse the term "the exchange" with the verb "to exchange." "To exchange" means to trade equal amounts of material, and is done usually without meaningful injury to either party.*

31.   fxg5   Ne5

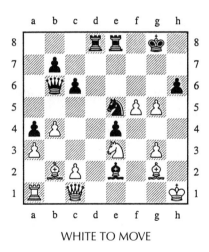

WHITE TO MOVE

Coolly played. Black seals the long diagonal with a temporary stopgap. The knight also eyeballs the squares f3, g4, and c4, any of which can be useful to Black when the timing is right. Throw in the open d-file for Black's queen-rook and the chance to invade White's heartland at d2 or d1 (if and when), and Black doesn't seem to be faring badly.

Look further, however, and you'll discover that White's king-side attacking threats still loom large. The once-dead bishop at b2 has become a menace. It reigns supreme on the a1-h8 diagonal. White's queen is ready to launch, too, and there lurks the possibility of obtaining dangerous connected passed pawns on the f- and g-files. Several other pieces could easily join the fray. Suddenly, a fully cocked attack force—a marauding army—could strike the denuded Black king.

In fact, Black could have faltered grievously on the previous move. If, instead of centralizing the knight by 31. . . . Nd7-e5, Deep Blue had materialistically expropriated the g-pawn with 31. . . . hxg5, White would have triumphed immediately by 32. Nd5 (or 32. Nc4), attacking the enemy queen. Capture the knight, 32. . . . cxd5, and White forces mate by 33. Qxg5 + .

As it is, White isn't down a full exchange. Kasparov has an extra pawn to boot, so that he's only behind by approximately one pawn (a rook, worth about five, for a bishop and pawn, to-gether worth about four).

32.   g6!   . . .

These are the connected passed pawns to which we've al-luded. Each pawn is capable of advancing with its partner's sup-port. One of them may reach the last rank, promoting to a new queen, compelling Black to surrender a minor piece or even a rook. White's invasive queen might be able to clasp onto one as an anchor for delivering mate. The possibilities aren't limitless, but they're sufficient.

32.   . . .   Bf3

Pinning the g2-bishop and protecting the e4-pawn. Black's not out of it yet.

33.   Bc3!   . . .

An ace realignment, securing d2 against an invasionary rook, while positioning the bishop itself on a safer square. These are the little moves that most of us never consider and great players somehow always find.

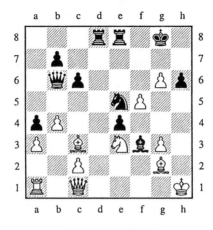

BLACK TO MOVE

33.   ...   Qb5

A new intrusion takes form. Deep Blue seeks deadly counter-play on the seventh rank, this time at e2 with the queen.

34.   Qf1   ...

No way, José. The champ stops it once and for all. Trade anyone?

34.   ...   Qxf1 +

35.   Rxf1   ...

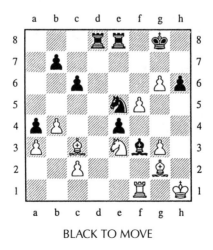

BLACK TO MOVE

The smoke has cleared, and it's time to step back and assess the position. In your own games, this is something you should do automatically—like Deep Blue—after anything significant has occurred. Here, the traffic-stopping incident is the exchange of queens, with its attendant entry into a new phase, the endgame.

On the surface, it may seem that White has chosen the wrong strategy in trading queens. One should seek piece exchanges when ahead in material, not when behind, because swapping down tends to emphasize the disparate ratio in favor of the stronger side. The more pieces you trade, the more important the remaining ones become. White is slightly behind in material, but by trading queens he blunts Black's attack and seizes the initiative.

The position contains other factors favorable to Kasparov, such as the connected passed pawns and the vulnerability of Black's king. The champion has rightly determined that he controls the play, and that's what counts. It's not just a matter of calculation, it has more to do with intuition and Kasparov's insightful grasp of position play.

35.   . . .   h5

Probably played to prevent the movement of White's g-pawn, before his kingside pawn roller becomes irresistible.

36.   Kg1   . . .

This activates the king, with the plan of bringing it to f2. His majesty is also relieved of the f3-bishop's pin, which frees his own light-square bishop for service at h3.

36.   . . .   Kf8

It's not clear that Black has to sidle the king so, or that very much is gained by moving it to f8. Perhaps one idea is to situate the king on e7, evacuating the eighth rank for rook activity.

37.   Bh3   . . .

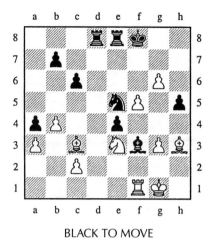

BLACK TO MOVE

Fights to enforce the advance g3-g4. If the h-file should open, White's rook can make a statement on h1, and Black's king will have to listen.

37.   ...   b5

Black deprives White of the ability to use c4, but that's not much relief at this juncture.

38.   Kf2   Kg7

Deep Blue decides to head for h6. The future doesn't look rosy there either.

39.   g4   ...

And now White plans to push the pawn to g5, to join its f5- and g6-partners in an awesome trio of trouble.

39.   ...   Kh6

40.   Rg1   ...

Renewing the threat to noodge ahead the g-pawn, this time with solid backup. Black must exchange pawns on g4.

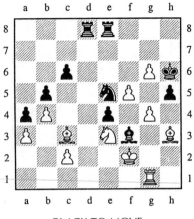

BLACK TO MOVE

40.	...	hxg4
41.	Bxg4	Bxg4
42.	Nxg4+	Nxg4+
43.	Rxg4	...

A lot of the wood has come off, and it's clear that Black can no longer thwart White's inexorable juggernaut. The final moves were:

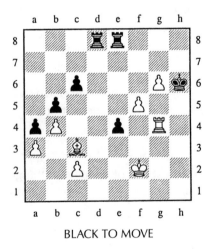

BLACK TO MOVE

43.	. . .	**Rd5**
44.	**f6**	**Rd1**
45.	**g7**	. . .

The pawns are unstoppable. White is going to promote by force, winning big material. So . . .

45.	. . .	**Black resigns (1–0)**

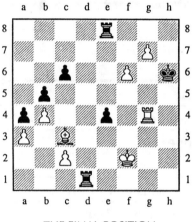

THE FINAL POSITION

Kasparov leads the match 1–0.

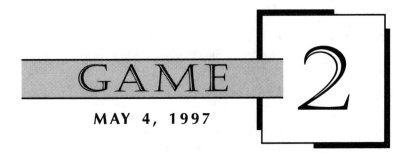

GAME 2

MAY 4, 1997

WHITE: **Deep Blue**

BLACK: **Garry Kasparov**

OPENING: **Ruy Lopez**

ECO CODE: **C93**

RESULT: **Deep Blue wins in 45 moves**

SCORE: **Kasparov 1—Deep Blue 1**

THE MOVES

NO.	WHITE	BLACK	NO.	WHITE	BLACK
1.	e4	e5	24.	Ra3	Rec8
2.	Nf3	Nc6	25.	Rca1	Qd8
3.	Bb5	a6	26.	f4	Nf6
4.	Ba4	Nf6	27.	fxe5	dxe5
5.	0-0	Be7	28.	Qf1	Ne8
6.	Re1	b5	29.	Qf2	Nd6
7.	Bb3	d6	30.	Bb6	Qe8
8.	c3	0-0	31.	R3a2	Be7
9.	h3	h6	32.	Bc5	Bf8
10.	d4	Re8	33.	Nf5	Bxf5
11.	Nbd2	Bf8	34.	exf5	f6
12.	Nf1	Bd7	35.	Bxd6	Bxd6
13.	Ng3	Na5	36.	axb5	axb5
14.	Bc2	c5	37.	Be4	Rxa2
15.	b3	Nc6	38.	Qxa2	Qd7
16.	d5	Ne7	39.	Qa7	Rc7
17.	Be3	Ng6	40.	Qb6	Rb7
18.	Qd2	Nh7	41.	Ra8 +	Kf7
19.	a4	Nh4	42.	Qa6	Qc7
20.	Nxh4	Qxh4	43.	Qc6	Qb6 +
21.	Qe2	Qd8	44.	Kf1	Rb8
22.	b4	Qc7	45.	Ra6	Black resigns
23.	Rec1	c4		(1–0)	

MACHINE BYTES BACK

Not to be outdone by the first game, Game 2 proved to be just as exciting, if not more so, full of unexpected moves and shifts. The real twist was that Deep Blue played like Kasparov, outlasting Garry in a strategic tug-of-war.

This time, the machine had White, starting with a two-square advance of the king-pawn. Kasparov countered symmetrically, moving out his king-pawn two squares also. Normally, he champions the aggressive Sicilian Defense, so this signaled a mindful, more deliberate approach.

Deep Blue essayed the Ruy Lopez, which affords White long-term initiative and pressure, but requires a sophisticated nursing of positional advantages. Thinking that he could outplay the machine in this kind of game, Kasparov continued in steadfast fashion, replying with the cautious Smyslov Variation on move nine.

But the computer never relinquished control, and by a meticulous buildup on the queenside, combined with a judicious opening of a second front on the kingside, compelled Kasparov to assume the unusual role of passive spectator.

Step by step, with precise maneuvering and timing, Deep Blue tightened the screws, until Black's defenses could no longer prevent a humbling intrusion. Faced with what appeared to be certain defeat, and perhaps chagrined by the machine's brilliant and subtle play, Kasparov failed to analyze an ingenious tactical resource and resigned on the 45th move in a position that could have led to perpetual check! What would Yogi say about this one?

White	**Black**
Deep Blue	Garry Kasparov

1.   e4   . . .

The most common opening move. The king-pawn lays claim to the center and releases the king-bishop and the queen.

1.   ...   e5

Black's retort is somewhat startling. Kasparov, king of the Sicilian Defense, undertakes a double king-pawn reply instead (both sides start by moving their e-pawns two squares).

By responding with the Sicilian (1. e4 c5), the defender aims for an asymmetrical setup, ceding some advantages to White, such as better development and greater attacking chances, in exchange for counterbalancers, such as more pawns in the middle and latent potential against the opponent's center.

With a double king-pawn reply, however, Black is taking a different stance. In effect he is saying, rather than take chances playing for a win, let's sit back and hold an equal position.

Of course, this is an oversimplification, and if Garry Kasparov has the opportunity, he will certainly take reasonable risks trying to win with the Black pieces. Moreover, it's possible to play a Sicilian Defense quietly and a double king-pawn sharply. Still, it's noteworthy that although these two answers to White's first move, c7-c5 (Sicilian), and e7-e5 (double KP), both fight for the square d4, they represent antithetical defensive philosophies.

2.   Nf3   Nc6

White attacks Black's e-pawn, and Black defends it. So far, nothing new under the sun.

3.   Bb5   ...

The Ruy Lopez, the most analyzed of all opening systems, some of the variations going more than forty moves deep. The reader might think that this confers an advantage on the machine, with its enormous opening book. Yet Kasparov knows these lines, too, perhaps even better than the voluminously gifted Deep Blue.

3.   ...   a6

Morphy's Defense, putting the question to the bishop. White can play the Exchange Variation, 4. Bxc6, doubling Black's

Some computers may be armed to their circuits, but how reliable are all these prefixed opening lines and evaluations? Not all of these appraisals come from top grandmasters and theoreticians, and even their assessments can be dubious or dead wrong.

The great world champion Emanuel Lasker, who reigned on Olympus for twenty-seven years (1894–1921), reputedly said that he could refute one out of every three of these variations. Sure, the art of analysis has improved tremendously since Lasker's day, but, thank goodness, we still make errors—all of us, even in today's multimedia world.

There's so much out there, too. Consider the Internet. How many inaccurate, corrupted, biased, wrong, or false ideas does it disseminate daily? How much of this is accepted as truth? Our data pool has been so infiltrated by mis- and disinformation, no one is safe from erroneous facts and valuations, not even masterful programmers and their Frankenstein creations, the supercomputers, which essentially do what they're told.

You must doubt the output if you can't trust the input. (Thank you, J. Cochran.)

pawns, or retreat the bishop to a4, maintaining the onslaught against the c6-knight.

Can White gain a pawn by removing the knight on c6 and then capturing the pawn on e5? It turns out that taking on c6 immediately doesn't win the e-pawn, for after 4. Bxc6 dxc6 5. Nxe5, Black gets the pawn back with a queen fork, 5. . . . Qd4.

Nonetheless, White could capture on c6 for positional reasons, so that when Black recaptures on c6 he accepts weaknesses (b7xc6) or an unfavorable pawn imbalance (d7xc6). To pose this dilemma to Black, however, White must relinquish a bishop for a knight. Unless specifically programmed in this case to take on c6, Deep Blue is not likely to surrender its valued bishop so early and lightly.

4. Ba4 ...

White withdraws the bishop, staying on the a4-e8 attacking diagonal. By continuing to assail the c6-knight, White's bishop really pressures what the knight guards—the pawn on e5. What's odd about this is that, by directly attacking a light square, c6, White's light-square bishop indirectly attacks a dark square, e5.

This adds another chapter to the bishop-and-knight saga. While it's true that bishops move along squares of one color only, they can influence squares of the other color by threatening knights that guard them.

4.   . . .   Nf6

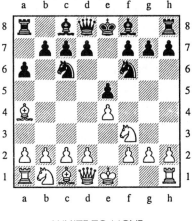

WHITE TO MOVE

Black develops the king-knight toward the center and begins the assault against White's king-pawn. Does White have to protect the e4-pawn?

5.   0-0   . . .

Not exactly. That is, not directly. By castling, White nestles his king safely at g1 and vacates e1 for the king-rook. White's king-pawn can be taken, Nf6xe4, introducing the Open Variation of the Ruy Lopez. But White has turnaround counterplay on the e-file against Black's uncastled king, with moves such as d2-d4 and Rf1-e1. In order to maintain a defensible position, Black will have to return the pawn.

A typical variation would be: 5. . . . Nxe4 6. d4 b5 7. Bb3 d5 8. dxe5 Be6. White has regained the pawn, but Black has closed the e-file, securing his king.

5.   ...   Be7

Black enters the Closed Variation of the Ruy Lopez instead. He places the king-bishop in front of the king for bulwark and prepares to castle. This development suggests that Kasparov (Black) felt he could better outplay the machine in a blocked, maneuvering position, where the concepts are more abstract and therefore harder to render into numerical evaluations.

Typically, computers do less well in these circumstances, preferring situations with open lines, in which ideas tend to be more concrete and essentially mathematical.

6.   Re1   ...

White secures its center, which finally threatens to gain Black's e-pawn, setting it up by first capturing the c6-knight. If Black were to castle, his pawn would fall to 7. Bxc6 dxc6 8. Nxe5, when Black's queen can no longer counterattack fertilely by moving to d4, the e5-knight being able to retreat to f3 with tempo.

6.   ...   b5

Now this is necessary to stave off the capture of the c6-knight.

7.   Bb3   d6

The champion solidifies his king-pawn and releases the queen-bishop for deployment. This also frees the queen-knight to chase the light-square bishop by edging to a5.

8.   c3   ...

The standard response, but also one in tune with Deep Blue's higher thought processes. It doesn't want to lose a bishop for a knight, so it gives the bishop a retreat square at c2. Moreover, c2-c3 supports the advance of the queen-pawn to d4.

8.   ...   0-0

The first part of the opening is over, with both sides having castled kingside. The next phase focuses on the center. White eyes the thrust d2-d4, exerting pressure against Black's king-pawn, and Black hopes to maintain a central presence, keeping and securing the counterweight at e5.

9.   h3   ...

Such a pawn move is often weakening and unnecessary, but here its function is to prevent Black's light-square bishop from moving to g4, pinning the f3-knight. White wants to insure that the knight's ability to fight for d4 and e5 continues unabated.

9.   . . .   h6

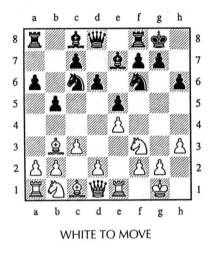

WHITE TO MOVE

This is the Smyslov Variation, named after the former Russian world-champion (1957–58) Vassily Smyslov. Stanley Kubrick, a chess fan and one of the strongest players in Hollywood, borrowed this surname for the film *2001*, ascribing it to the chief Soviet scientist who visits the space station.

The idea behind h7-h6 is to protect g5, so that Black's king-rook can move without hazard. Otherwise, with Black's rook at e8, White's f3-knight might jump to g5, pestering f7 in tandem with the b3-bishop.

More common ninth moves for Black are the Breyer Variation, retreating the queen-knight to b8, to reposition to d7; the Zaitsev Variation, flanking the queen-bishop at b7, clearing the home rank while targeting d5 and e4; and the most analyzed of all, the Chigorin Variation, shifting the queen-knight to a5, flailing at White's bishop.

10.   d4   . . .

With this move, Deep Blue obtains lebensraum for its pieces and starts to turn up the heat on Black's king-pawn.

> *You have an edge in space if you control more of the board than your opponent, but this isn't always easy to determine. Sometimes it's simpler just to look at the middle. If your center pawns are farther advanced than your opponent's, you're probably spatially ahead, with more room behind the lines to shift and reposition.*

The world champion has chosen a defensive setup that allows White steady, long-term pressure. Admittedly, Deep Blue's advantage is minimal, and Black has a perfectly fine game in this book line. Most machines, in fact, fare badly when circumstances dictate a patient, maneuvering approach. But this is no ordinary computer, as Kasparov soon discovers.

10.   ...   Re8

Adding protection to e5 and clearing f8 for the dark-square bishop.

11.   Nbd2   ...

Since c3 is blocked, the knight is developed to the less ambitious d2. Its scope is reduced on this square, but from d2 it's often possible to redirect the knight to active posts across the frontier line, at f5 and d5. The knight can reach either square by going from d2 to f1 to e3 and beyond. It can also attain f5 by jumping from f1 to g3 instead.

Inexperienced players are loath to play a move like Nbd2, thinking that it obstructs the bishop at c1. This is true, but the obstruction is temporary and not serious. In this congested position, it's unclear where to put the c1-bishop anyhow, so why not wait for more clues to come in?

11.   ...   Bf8

The anticipated retreat, unveiling the e8-rook's defense to e5.

12.   Nf1   Bd7

Deep Blue pursues its programmed layout, and Kasparov also follows the known variation, clearing the home rank and securing c6. In this uninspired line, it's difficult to see how Black is going to drum up play.

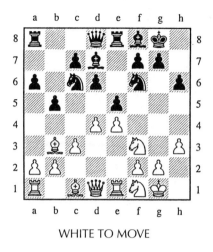

WHITE TO MOVE

Mere mortals might have blundered, trying to pilfer a pawn by 12. . . . exd4 13. cxd4 Nxe4? (or 13. . . . Rxe4 14. Rxe4 Nxe4), when White has a nasty rejoinder, Bb3-d5, forking and skewering Black's soft spots at a8, c6, and e4. This tactic is fairly common in Ruy Lopez lines where Black weakens the a8-h1 diagonal by playing b7-b5, and then avariciously pockets the e-pawn.

13. Ng3 . . .

This strengthens the e-pawn and observes f5. Moreover, the side-by-side knights on f3 and g3 provide shelter and support for the White king. It's good to have friends.

13. . . . Na5

Black gains time to move up the c-pawn by assailing the b3-bishop. Both the computer and the given book line are in favor of spending the tempo to keep the bishop.

14. Bc2 . . .

This is too worthy a bishop to let go. It guards the e-pawn, lords it over f5, and if an exchange ever takes place, resulting in e4xd5, suddenly it metamorphoses to bug the kingside. It may later on even go back to reign on the a2-g8 diagonal.

This type of Ruy Lopez position for White plays itself. According to the famed Russian grandmaster David Bronstein: "It's like milking a cow."

14.   ...   c5

Black's rejoinder attacks d4 and clears c7 for the queen, so that it can unblock the home rank and stand sentinel over e5.

15.   b3   ...

White plays this to keep the a5-knight out of c4, not to flank the queen-bishop, which is improved by being on e3. Since all of these moves are part of the literature on this opening, Kasparov has not yet had the opportunity to steer the game into uncharted waters, to get the machine on its own. He's still playing against the accumulated knowledge of the entire world, or something like that.

The debate continues. Who has the edge in situations like this? The best human chess player, with his ability to creatively find new paths, or a chess-playing supercomputer, with its limitless data banks and ability to jump to light speed through 200 million positions per second? Human vs. machine, individual intelligence vs. collective intelligence—you decide.

15.   ...   Nc6

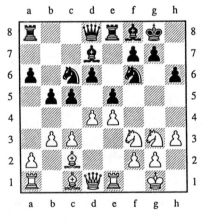

WHITE TO MOVE

Now that Black has moved up his c-pawn to attack White's d-pawn, he can bring the wild horse back to c6, this time behind the c-pawn instead of in front of it.

A machine moment has been reached. Will it opt to keep the lines open by exchanging pawns on c5, or will it lock up the center by advancing the queen-pawn to d5? Two radically different positions, requiring diverse talents to play.

16.   d5   . . .

Two diametrically opposed types of positions are the open and the closed. Generally, they are open or closed because of the central pawn formation.

The center is open if it is unblocked by pawns of either color, to the extent that pieces can freely move through it and possibly occupy the center squares. The center is closed if it is blocked by pawns of both colors, so that neither side can pass through it or occupy any of the middle squares.

These two types of centers require different strategies. With an open center (or open game or open position) you should rely on your pieces, attacking the enemy king's position and forcing the opponent to accept weaknesses. Since the center is unimpeded, things can happen quite quickly, so king safety is paramount. It's from these kinds of situations that sudden mating attacks tend to spring.

Play in a closed center (or closed game or closed position) is dissimilar. Here the middle is usually blocked by interlocking White and Black pawns, so that activity must take place on the flanks, or just off the center. Things don't happen as quickly, so that one has more time to develop a plan with careful maneuvering and redeployments. King safety is not as important a factor, since sudden mating attacks are not likely to materialize when forces can't penetrate the middle.

Generally, though not exclusively, open games tend to be more tactical and calculating, whereas closed games are more likely to be strategic and intuitive. Since computers tend to be brute-force wizards, while humans are past masters of intuition, computers should prefer open games over closed.

The Rubicon is crossed. Deep Blue shuts the door in the center, changing the character of the position indelibly into a closed game. Since humans generally outplay computers in closed situations, which are more intuitive and require greater comprehension, the machine's strategy seems awry.

But here, Deep Blue has elected to enter upon a path that the world champion has visited far more often. What does this mean? Why is there something rather than nothing?

16.   . . .   Ne7

Black gets the knight out of attack, with the idea of transferring it to the kingside. Already we see that the cramped position necessitates maneuvering behind the lines.

17.   Be3   . . .

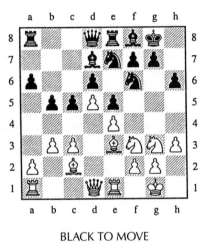

BLACK TO MOVE

It took seventeen moves, but the bishop has found a home, a comfortable one at that. In this closed position, White has a minimal spatial advantage based on its farther-advanced center pawn at d5. Note Black's tight quarters and the huddling together of his forces in the middle. Will he be squeezed to death or will his potential energy explode to kinetic?

17.   . . .   Ng6

The knight takes residence on the kingside, with the possibility of mooring at f4. With so much breastwork on the kingside,

Black's king looks especially safe. The big loser might be Black's dark-square bishop, whose movement is impeded by its own center pawns.

Activity seems to be freighted toward the kingside, where Kasparov is armed and on alert. But what about the queenside?

18.   Qd2   . . .

Connecting the rooks and doubling on the c1-h6 diagonal, though with no real threats. With spatial superiority, however, comes greater coordination. White can probably switch to the queenside faster than Black. Now that White's rooks support each other, the computer must be considering the push a2-a4, with the idea of opening the a-file, when desirable, by exchanging on b5. Should Black prepare to meet this riposte?

18.   . . .   Nh7

Black withdraws the knight to unblock the d8-h4 diagonal, allowing the g6-knight to invade on h4 with the queen's support, offering to trade knights. By exchanging pieces, Kasparov might relieve some of the congestion. From h7, the knight may also have the opportunity to jump to g5 to exert pressure against White's kingside.

But maybe the queenside should have been brought into focus. The champion might have anticipated White's next move by advancing his rook-pawn to a5.

19.   a4!   . . .

If Black had played a6-a5 on the previous move, he would now have sufficient protection on the square b4 to answer White's a2-a4 by pushing past, b5-b4. But he didn't play a6-a5, and b4 is not guarded enough, so Kasparov cannot keep the queenside closed.

19.   . . .   Nh4

Kasparov's last move follows the plan of swapping knights. These would be the first captures of the game, on move twenty. In the first game, nothing was taken until move nineteen. Are we seeing a strategy here?

Deep Blue has the edge, but it's not Anatoly Karpov, Kasparov's longtime rival and a true maestro of the closed game. Can a mere machine play this kind of game intelligently, cultivating its positional advantages? Until this game, few thought so.

20.   Nxh4   Qxh4

21.   Qe2   . . .

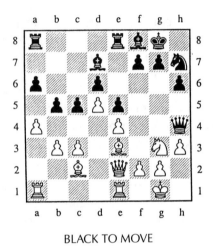

BLACK TO MOVE

A two-headed move. Toward the queenside, White retains a predator's eye on b5. On the kingside, the queen lines up for passage to h5 to offer a queen trade, in case Black's offensive there starts to go somewhere.

If Black now tries to keep the a-file closed by b5-b4, White will exchange on b4 and push to a5, leaving Black with assailable pawns on b4 and a6.

21.   . . .   Qd8

Time to beat a retreat. Black chooses to redeploy the queen for defensive duty on the queenside.

22.   b4   . . .

Fixing b5 as a target.

22.   . . .   Qc7

Black reconnects the rooks and hopes to manufacture play on the queen-bishop file.

23.   Rec1!   . . .

This is not a computer's move, at least not until now. It's the kind of move a nurturing positional player might find, not a tactical automaton. It doesn't seem to do much, but it carries with it latent sting and promise. Suddenly, Kasparov must worry about White's looming advance of the c-pawn, supported menacingly by the c1-rook.

23.   . . .   c4

The champion chooses to close the c-file, negating White's possibilities on it, but destroying his own chances for counterplay along the same route. Thus, the only line that could become open on the queenside is the a-file, and Deep Blue's in charge of that.

24.   Ra3!   . . .

This proves it. In order to control the a-file, White first doubles rooks behind the a-pawn before exchanging on b5. It's a standard strategic artifice, usually employed by masterful position players, and now apparently a ruse in the repertoire of Deep Blue. If Black is to maintain a counterstance on this file, he must insure that the a8-rook is satisfactorily supported, preferably by his other rook and the queen.

24.   . . .   Rec8

Black envisions a defense in which the a8-rook is guarded twice, by the king-rook at c8 and the queen at d8. This works because the queen is the third major piece (queen or rook) in line along the home rank. It would therefore be the last piece to retake on a8, avoiding capture itself.

25.   Rca1   . . .

Completing the doubling maneuver. The threat is to take on b5, and Black will be unable to recapture with the a-pawn, it being pinned as a shield to the a8-rook.

25.   . . .   Qd8

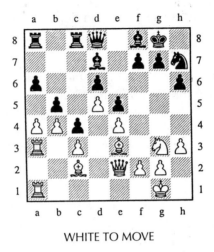

WHITE TO MOVE

Black defends a8 for the second time. If 26. axb5 axb5 27. Rxa8 Rxa8 28. Rxa8, Black can recapture with the queen, seizing control of the a-file. Nice work if you can get it.

Another tack would be to decline taking on a8, instead invading on a7. After 26. axb5 axb5 27. Ra7, however, Black can hold the fort by exchanging rooks, 27. . . . Rxa7 28. Rxa7, followed by opposing rooks once more, 28. . . . Ra8. This thwarts the incursion.

Back to our theme. It's move twenty-six, and all the pawns are still on the board. The only line about to open is the a-file. White needs to hatch a second plot, to divert Black's attention and to acquire another port of entry.

26.   f4!   . . .

At this time, White can't break through fruitfully on the a-file. By creating a fresh point of attack, however, it might eventually be able to use its superior mobility to lure Black out of position, or into a situation where the threats to both areas can't be guarded simultaneously. For instance, by feinting toward one, Black could be lured out of position, unable to honor his defensive commitment to the other.

26.   . . .   Nf6

Black brings his knight back into the game. If White takes on e5, Black can retake with the d-pawn, vacating d6 for the knight, which could springboard there from e8. At d6 the knight would be an excellent blockader, preventing the d-pawn's advance, while attacking over the obstructive pawns.

Black, of course, doesn't take the bishop-pawn, 26. . . . e5xf4, for after White takes back, White's knight could later be repositioned at d4, a commanding base of operations, with a beautiful overlook of Black's fortifications.

27. fxe5 dxe5

The first pawn exchanges of the game, and they leave White with a half-open f-file (White's rooks can use it, Black's can't) and a protected passed pawn at d5. Protected passed pawns are useful, because they don't need piece protection in the endgame, being already guarded by a pawn, thus freeing the friendly king to pursue aggressive plans elsewhere. On Black's side of the ledger is the ability to use d6 for blockade.

28. Qf1 . . .

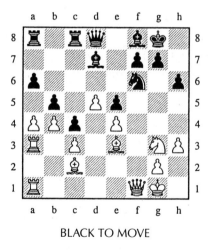

BLACK TO MOVE

There seem to be two points to this move, aimed at two different fronts. On the queenside, White prepares shifting the queen to a1, after the a1-rook has moved to a2. That would triple major pieces along the a-file and go a long way toward dominating the line.

On the kingside, the reason for Qe2-f1 is tactical. If ever exchanges take place on a8, deflecting Black's queen from the defense of f6, White could take the king-rook pawn, Be3xh6, undermining protection for f6. White's queen would then be able to capture the knight on f6.

These are the ideas, but admittedly Qe2-f1 looks somewhat unwieldy. Perhaps better would simply have been to double on the a7-g1 diagonal by Qe2-f2.

28.   ...   Ne8

The expected continuation to Black's plan. The knight is headed for the blockade square at d6.

29.   Qf2   ...

What's this? Has the machine changed its collective mind? Or did the transfer of the knight to e8 change the game's dynamic? Anyway, by overprotecting the a7-g1 diagonal, White's dark-square bishop is suddenly loaded to invade on b6.

29.   ...   Nd6

On d6, the knight becomes Black's most effective piece, giving Kasparov the best deal for his money. Compare it to his major pieces and dark-square bishop, which are sitting passively, waiting for Godot.

30.   Bb6   ...

Seizing useful queenside squares and driving Black's queen to e8, if the double guard on a8 is to be kept.

30.   ...   Qe8

31.   R3a2?   ...

What? I'm okay, how are you? There must be some deep—very deep—tactical reason for this retreat, hidden in the recesses of Deep Blue's scheming mind. The only thing I can see is that, at 200 million positions per second, the machine determined that, once b5 is clear, the d6-knight might be able to move to b5, forking the rook on a3 and the pawn on c3. I think we have to respect that judgment.

31. ... Be7

Kasparov naturally tries to activate his foundering king-bishop, but this placement interferes with the queen's defense to e5. Moreover, on e7, the bishop can be attacked by a knight from f5. Black's position, with its lack of space, has a corresponding paucity of possibilities.

32. Bc5 Bf8?

Wow. This is reminiscent of Game 1, when Deep Blue repeated moves, shifting its bishop from d6 to c7 and back to d6. But here it appears that the human is aping the machine. However you peel it, the champ is wasting time. With the computer in command, this is a luxury Kasparov may not have.

33. Nf5! ...

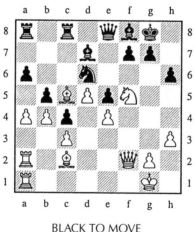

BLACK TO MOVE

Playing to get the advantage of two bishops. Moreover, if Black's d7-bishop takes the knight, White's e-pawn will take back, increasing the diagonal power of White's light-square bishop.

Since computers love bishops, and since Deep Blue is a computer (we're beginning to wonder), it must be incredibly desirous of making this transaction.

33. ... Bxf5

> *Bishops tend to be stronger than knights in a majority of circumstances. Two friendly bishops usually gain even more in utility when they work as a unit, opposed by a bishop and knight or two knights, particularly because each bishop can make up for the other's weakness—the inability to control squares of the other color.*
>
> *As an aligned team they can imperiously govern consecutive diagonals, or centrally crossing ones, conferring a huge spatial edge, especially against two enemy knights. If you possess this type of superiority, it is said that you have "the two bishops," or "two bishops," or "the two-bishop advantage."*

Black eliminates White's pesky knight, giving up his bishop and retaining his own knight, which is necessary to keep the position blockaded.

34.   exf5   f6

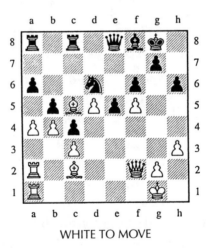

WHITE TO MOVE

A natural move, to secure the king-pawn and to prevent the advance of White's f-pawn. Unfortunately, it weakens the light squares (e6 and g6) and worsens the condition of Black's dark-square bishop. It also lets White exchange down, enabling the computer's queen to invade on b6. In the end, this proves crucial. Black might have guarded b6 here by Qe8-d8, keeping the status quo and living to enjoy another day.

35.   Bxd6   ...

Beginning a series of exchanges to insure an allied landing on Black's beaches. Deep Blue's D-Day timing is perfect.

35.   ...   Bxd6

36.   axb5   axb5

37.   Be4   ...

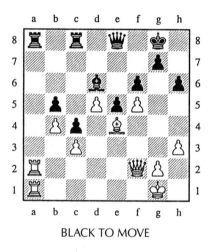

BLACK TO MOVE

A strong positional move, played to obstruct e5, preventing Black from obtaining activity by advancing the e-pawn. A more materialistic, computerlike idea, however, was to invade with the queen on b6. But the variations stemming from this are wild, and Deep Blue must have decided that Qf2-b6 might lead to an ending with bishops of opposite colors, reducing the chances to win, even with a material advantage.

> *Endings of opposite-color bishops (one bishop travels on light squares, while the opponent's bishop moves on dark squares) are notoriously drawn, even when one side is ahead by a pawn or two. This is so because the inferior side may be able to set up an unbreakable blockade on the squares not guarded by the enemy bishop.*

37.   ...   Rxa2

38.   Qxa2   ...

White correctly takes back with the queen to double major pieces on the a-file, maintaining continued use of the line. Taking back with the rook, Ra1xa2, would allow Black to neutralize White's hold with Rc8-a8. By opposing rooks, Black forestalls the invasion.

38.   ...   Qd7

Black can no longer cancel out White on the a-file, so Kasparov draws the line on his second rank. This is not his type of game, merely trying to stitch things together. Step by step, Deep Blue has demonstrated strategic understanding, something no computer has ever done before, on its way to outplaying the greatest chess champion of all time.

39.   Qa7   ...

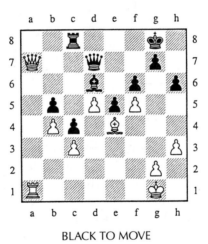

BLACK TO MOVE

Occupying the seventh rank. Black must tread carefully. Should he exchange queens, trying to salvage the endgame by using his opposite-color bishop to set up a blockade, or should he avoid a queen trade, hoping to save the day by conjuring counterplay?

39.   ...   Rc7

Kasparov's indomitable fighting spirit works against him, and he winds up shooting himself in the foot. Now White's queen starts to be more than annoying.

40. Qb6 ...

Menacing the b-pawn and clearing the way for the rook's entrance.

40. ... Rb7

41. Ra8+ Kf7

Black's king might have found greater shelter at h7, but he'd also be farther from the action. A mistake would be to block the check by 41. . . . Bd6-b8. White's rook could win the bishop with check, protected by the queen, in x-ray fashion, through Black's rook. If 41. . . . Bf8, then 42.d6! wins.

42. Qa6 ...

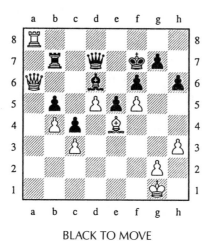

BLACK TO MOVE

White has changed the relative positions of his rook and queen along the a-file. Before, the queen was ahead of the rook; now, the rook is in front of the queen. That's a neat maneuver, whether artificially, humanly, or divinely inspired.

42. ... Qc7

43. Qc6! ...

Offering to trade queens, obtaining a dangerous passed pawn and increasing the light-square bishop's scope in the process.

43.   ...   Qb6 +

44.   Kf1   ...

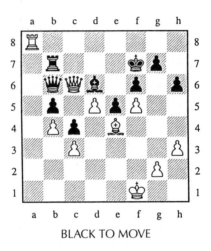

BLACK TO MOVE

A tough choice. Deep Blue moves the king closer to the center, instead of to h1, thinking that this offered more chances to offset the possibility of a perpetual check, in case Black's queen tried a last-ditch excursion to e3.

44.   ...   Rb8

45.   Ra6!   ...

Crushing, right? Kasparov thought so, as did almost every commentator there, and the world champion graciously gave up.

45.   ...   Black resigns (1–0)

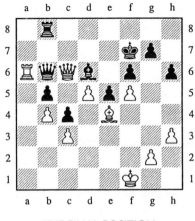

THE FINAL POSITION

The game's greatest player had been outgeneraled in a positional masterpiece. Funny thing is, the final position is drawn.

The drawing idea was found by several analysts within hours of the game's end. In fact, most strong players considered the initial part of the variation but didn't take the analysis far enough, rejecting its drawing promise. They too were fooled. It seems they thought that if Deep Blue allowed it, the drawing line couldn't work. And if Kasparov resigned, the game must be lost! Mass delusion, brought on by computer reverence.

The champ missed or undervalued 45. . . . Qe3!. After 46. Qxd6, Black must answer 46. . . . Re8!. There are several variants that White could try, but they all seem to lead to a draw. Perhaps the most representative one is: 47. h4! Qxe4! 48. Ra7 + Kg8 49. Qd7 Qf4 + 50. Kg1 Qe3 + 51. Kh2 Qf4 + 52. Kh3 Re7! 53. Qc8 + Kh7 54. Rxe7 h5! 55. Rxg7 + Kxg7 56. Qd7 + Kh6, when Black has perpetual threats in hand.

In human, all too human fashion, Garry Kasparov, impressed by the machine's stellar performance, and having to hold on precariously for the final third of the game, must have been beaten psychologically! He thought he was lost, so he gave up. He apparently had forgotten the wonderful aphorism of grand-

master and teacher Dr. Savielly Tartakower (1887–1956), who supposedly remarked: "No one ever won a game by resigning."
The match is tied 1–1.

Perpetual check is a way to draw, by which the inferior side can give a series of checks that do not produce mate, but that cannot be stopped. No progress can be made, and the defender saves the game.

Either the players agree to a draw or the game is drawn by three-fold repetition, where the same position occurs at three points with the same player to move. The side trying to salvage the game will claim a draw by announcing his intention to repeat the position for the third time before he actually does so.

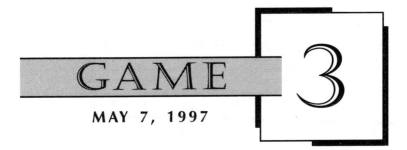

GAME 3

MAY 7, 1997

WHITE: **Garry Kasparov**

BLACK: **Deep Blue**

OPENING: **English Opening by transposition**

ECO CODE: **A28**

RESULT: **Draw in 48 moves**

SCORE: **Kasparov 1.5—Deep Blue 1.5**

THE MOVES

NO.	WHITE	BLACK	NO.	WHITE	BLACK
1.	d3	e5	25.	f5	Qxd1
2.	Nf3	Nc6	26.	Bxd1	Bh7
3.	c4	Nf6	27.	Nh3	Rfb8
4.	a3	d6	28.	Nf4	Bd8
5.	Nc3	Be7	29.	Nfd5	Nc6
6.	g3	0-0	30.	Bf4	Ne5
7.	Bg2	Be6	31.	Ba4	Nxd5
8.	0-0	Qd7	32.	Nxd5	a5
9.	Ng5	Bf5	33.	Bb5	Ra7
10.	e4	Bg4	34.	Kg2	g5
11.	f3	Bh5	35.	Bxe5+	dxe5
12.	Nh3	Nd4	36.	f6	Bg6
13.	Nf2	h6	37.	h4	gxh4
14.	Be3	c5	38.	Kh3	Kg8
15.	b4	b6	39.	Kxh4	Kh7
16.	Rb1	Kh8	40.	Kg4	Bc7
17.	Rb2	a6	41.	Nxc7	Rxc7
18.	bxc5	bxc5	42.	Rxa5	Rd8
19.	Bh3	Qc7	43.	Rf3	Kh8
20.	Bg4	Bg6	44.	Kh4	Kg8
21.	f4	exf4	45.	Ra3	Kh8
22.	gxf4	Qa5	46.	Ra6	Kh7
23.	Bd2	Qxa3	47.	Ra3	Kh8
24.	Ra2	Qb3	48.	Ra6	Draw
					($^1/_2$–$^1/_2$)

DRAWN BY INFERENCE

S till trying to confuse his opponent, Kasparov starts with the Mieses Opening, a debut perhaps never seen before in a championship-caliber event. It soon transposes into an English Opening. Deep Blue responds with straightforward development and concern for the center.

A sidebar to Kasparov's strategy is that he tries to lure the machine into defending with a setup that White normally obtains in the Sicilian Defense, but with Deep Blue being a full move behind. The electronic wonder doesn't buy it, instead opting to keep the center closed and to develop further.

But it does seem that Deep Blue is misled. Losing its way, it begins to station pieces awkwardly, and the champion gets a positional edge. To counter this superiority, the machine does what it does best. It tries to snatch a pawn, and Kasparov lets the pawn go, hoping to derive a stronger attack.

Deep Blue defends with acumen, actually forcing the exchange of queens and simplifying to an endgame. But it's not so simple. Kasparov keeps his potent position even with the queens off the board. So Deep Blue decides to give the material back to break the attack.

After equalizing the game, Kasparov retains some advantage in position, but the machine finds just enough counterpressure against the champion's backward center pawn to prevent progress from being made. Kasparov proposes a draw on move 48 and Deep Blue's blue-ribbon team accepts.

White	Black
Garry Kasparov	Deep Blue

1.   d3   . . .

The Mieses Opening, named after the German grandmaster Jacques Mieses (1865–1954), and to my knowledge, never played in a world-championship-type event before. It may be the first time Kasparov has attempted it in public. Several of my students thrive on it, but none of them are about to challenge Garry.

Obviously, Kasparov wanted to confuse Deep Blue, hoping to get it out of book knowledge with dispatch. Nonetheless, I suspect that Deep Blue knows about this beginning move too. The machine's chief chess adviser, grandmaster Joel Benjamin, an acknowledged connoisseur of offbeat lines, has even published an informed volume on them.

1.   . . .   e5

Deep Blue responds to Kasparov's creeping policy by direct occupation of the center.

2.   Nf3   . . .

One thing about White's initial move, d2-d3, is that it guards e4. So now, with Black's king-pawn imperiled, the Deep Blue sea can't turn the attack around. If the king-pawn pushed ahead to harass White's knight, White would then take it for free.

There's another point to Kasparov's unusual beginning. By a clever transposition, he may be able to dupe the machine into accepting a position known to be unfavorable to Black.

To transpose moves means to establish the same setup by playing the moves that lead to it in a different sequence. One position is a transposition of another if it is the same (or nearly the same) position, but results from a different move order.

By transposing moves, you might catch your opponent off guard, especially if he's playing the first few moves mechanically. If he's a complete tin man, maybe you can hoodwink him into entering a variation he'd otherwise avoid.

Another possibility is that by playing your moves in different order, you may prevent your opponent from reaching his desired array. Meanwhile, if the transposition works, you get your dream position anyway.

Geniuses like Garry Kasparov—maybe there have been five or six in history—are keenly aware of such opportunities, rarely missing the chance to so cozen their opponents.

2.   ...   Nc6

Defending the pawn without yet moving the d-pawn, so that Black retains the option of moving it two squares.

3.   c4   ...

By advancing the c-pawn, White essentially transposes into the English Opening, which normally comes about when White plays c2-c4 on the first move.

In English formations, White aims to control the light squares in the center. This plan is usually aided by the fianchetto of the kingside bishop at g2. The central light squares also come under the sway of a knight from c3 and pawns at c4 and d3. To this extent we say that, in the English Opening, White plays a light-square game.

3.   ...   Nf6

Black develops the king-knight toward the center and prepares the possibility of mobilizing the d-pawn two squares. That would open the middle and make Black's position similar in appearance to White's in the Sicilian Defense.

4.   a3   ...

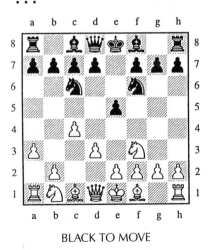

BLACK TO MOVE

By this little push, Kasparov is offering Deep Blue the chance to go into a Sicilian Defense in reverse, with White having Black's typical position and Black getting White's. This transformation could be achieved if Deep Blue advances the d-pawn two squares and White takes it with his c-pawn.

But why would Garry Kasparov, Mr. Attack, forfeit the White positions for the more defensive Black ones? The answer is that, though he would obtain a Black alignment, he would do so with an additional move in hand, which presumably could be employed productively. Meanwhile, Black would arrive at White's deployment, but a move behind!

The thinking is, since legitimate Black defenses and formations should be good enough to draw, they must be clearly advantageous if obtained with an extra move still to play. And if Black has White's arrangement, but a move behind, his position should be deficient in some way. At least, that's the theory behind it.

What's really going on here is that Kasparov is still trying to confuse the computer with unorthodoxy, perhaps hoping to catch Deep Blue in an unfavorable transposition.

Superficially, this strategy seems logical, but actually it might have greater application against another human. Anthropoids are more likely to be confounded or caught napping. Computers, on the other manufactured hand, are fortified with all kinds of cross-checks and safeguards. They look at everything, they make constant comparisons, they recognize patterns uncannily, and they usually don't fall asleep.

It's hard not to admire Kasparov's wily strategy, trying to arrive at positions in which he can exercise his greater intuition and positional grasp. But, in hindsight, maybe his chances wouldn't have been impaired if he had ventured the usual bold and brilliant style. It's done rather well up to now.

4.   . . .   d6

Deep Blue spurns the offer! It chooses not to assume the White side of a Sicilian, colors reversed and a move behind. Instead it opts to play a more cautious game, overprotecting its e-pawn and opening the diagonal for the light-square bishop.

5.   Nc3   . . .

White continues with his light-square game, and now Black should pursue a dark-square plan. The mechanical one's queen-knight, and d- and e-pawns observe dark squares. In support of these deployments, it makes sense to flank Black's king-bishop at g7. From there, eventually the bishop will influence key squares at midcourt and achieve superior scope.

5.   . . .   Be7

Now this is a perfunctory move. It's clearly the wrong place for the dark-square bishop. It belongs at g7, not behind the lines at e7, where its mobility is hardly preferable to that of a pawn.

6.   g3   . . .

Kasparov starts a kingside fianchetto, to buoy up his light-square layout through the board's midsection.

6.   . . .   0-0

The curtain has come down on the first act. Deep Blue is safely castled and ready to pick up the action.

7.   Bg2   Be6

From e6 the bishop is ambidextrous. It watches over d5 and also views the kingside, particularly the potential invasion square h3. The only thing it must be heedful of, for now, is an attack from the f3-knight at g5.

8.   0-0   . . .

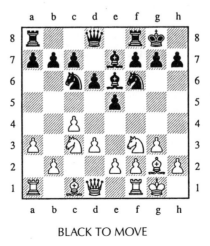

BLACK TO MOVE

White castles too. Food for thought: his formation resembles the Black side of the Dragon Variation of the Sicilian Defense. Why is it called the Dragon? Supposedly, if you trace the outline of White's pieces and pawns across the board, and if you have a vivid imagination, it looks like St. George's imaginary beast, with its serpentine tail. How sinuous can things get?

8.   ...   Qd7?

Where is Siegfried when you need him? Deep Blue wants to support the invasion of the light-square bishop to h3, to slay White's valued king-bishop. Such an exchange would weaken the light squares around White's king. But the real monster is White's king-knight, which now leaps to g5, breathing fire at Black's e6-bishop, while still keeping a tailhold on h3, preventing invasion.

Instead of 8. . . . Qd7, Black should first have played its king-rook pawn to h6. This would guard g5, keeping out White's knight, after which Black could develop the queen to d7 on the ensuing move. In chess, as in life, timing matters.

9.   Ng5   ...

White besets the bishop and gains time to move up the f-pawn, which the knight had been blocking. Moreover, the knight also defends h3 against intrusion, preserving White's fianchet-toed bishop.

Another way for White to keep his flanked bishop, instead of moving the knight to g5, is to shunt the rook to e1. When Black's bishop then intrudes on h3, White could draw his own bishop back to h1, it no longer being pinned to the rook. But that course is less aggressive and unsuited to Kasparov's taste.

9.   ...   Bf5

The supercomputer elects to hold onto its bishop. Nothing surprising about that. The machine possibly reckoned that it would be deleterious to White's position to attack the bishop again by moving the king-pawn to e4.

How does Deep Blue decide on its moves, anyway?

Deep Blue determines its moves by computing an arithmetic score, evaluating each position in terms of four variables: pieces, position, king safety, and tempo. The move played is the one with the highest positive tally. A move's score can also be negative, and it's typically expressed in hundredths of points (for instance, -1.08 or $+.73$).

Pawns start with a value of one point, and the other pieces are assigned values based on the pawn. Thus knights and bishops are worth about three pawns each, with bishops having a slight edge in a majority of positions. Rooks are worth five pawns and queens nine. The king's exchange value is set ridiculously high, even though it has a movement value of only four pawns, since its loss entails losing the game. The value of each unit is modified during the course of play, based on placement and utility.

The position factor has to do with mobility and space. Values are allocated based on the number of squares a piece controls and its ability to use them. For example, a piece might be in line to move somewhere, but not safely.

King safety speaks for itself. The computer evaluates the relative risks and options of the two kings. In its formulations it seeks moves that endanger the enemy king and safeguard its own.

The tempo element obviously relates to time. Deep Blue tries not to waste moves, developing pieces to the right squares, implementing plans expeditiously, and completing tasks with economy, without excess force or loss of tempi.

Deep Blue generally tries to augment its own possibilities while counteracting and reducing the opponent's potential. Its parallel thinking capabilities enable it to reckon all these diverse calculations simultaneously, integrating them with other considerations and features to arrive at an overall plus or minus value. The computer then plays the move with the greatest positive number.

Kasparov would do it differently, but his way works too.

10.   e4   ...

Kasparov, however, determines that the problems of this move, e2-e4, are more than offset by what he gets in compensation. What White gains is a tempo, with the threat to Black's bishop, and staunch control of the square d5, which tends to be White's chief focus in the English.

The drawbacks are that the g2-bishop is barred from using the a8-h1 diagonal, at least for now, and White forfeits the ability to guard d4 with a pawn. Since no White pawn can attack d4, Black might be able to occupy that square to advantage, especially with a knight.

But all things considered, White maintains the initiative and the energy needed to direct the flow of play. This is what generally counts the most in chess.

10.   ...   Bg4

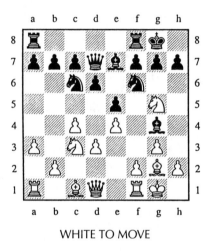

WHITE TO MOVE

Black pesters the queen but doesn't gain a move, for White gets it back by blocking the threat with a counterattack, so the bishop will have to move again anyway.

11.   f3   ...

White may want to move his f-pawn (to attack the center and to activate the f1-rook), but to f4, not f3, so this represents a temporary delay in plans. The block is necessary, however, so that White can maintain the initiative.

11.   ...   Bh5

By this retreat, Black keeps the f3-pawn pinned to the queen, and therefore unable to shoot farther ahead to hit the center. Via some clever maneuvering, however, not uncharacteristic of the

English Opening, White might be able to recharge the f-pawn's push and reconstitute order in the ranks.

Black must stay mindful of its h5-bishop. With White's pawns capable of a sudden outburst, Deep Blue must make sure its bishop doesn't get enmeshed and trapped in a kingside fusillade.

12.   Nh3   . . .

Not an atypical retreat, with the idea of transferring the knight to f2, though this is not yet imperative. White might have waited for Black to weaken its kingside with h7-h6, trying to drive away the knight. Perhaps more in tune with the spirit of the opening is the simple development Bc1-e3, clearing the queenside and

---

Newcomers are often confused by the concepts of winning material (or losing it) and trading material. You win material when you get more than you give up. You trade when you get the same (in value) as you give up.

Thus, if you surrender a pawn to capture a rook, you've won material. Since a rook is worth five and a pawn one, you've gained about four points (or pawns) in value. But if you take the enemy queen with your queen, and then your queen is taken back, you haven't lost a queen. You've traded queens, nine points for nine (or, since values are expressed in pawns, nine pawns for nine pawns).

Generally, you should reject out of hand making a transaction that loses material, unless there are ancillary gains. For example, you might deem it wise to lose (sacrifice) a pawn for positional dominance. But you wouldn't want to win a queen if it led to your being mated next move.

Otherwise, winning (or losing) material is straightforward. You simply compare what you get to what you give up.

A trade is different. You can't resolve to make a trade based solely on immediate material concerns, because no one gains or loses in the bargain. You'd need to consult additional elements as well, such as time, space, pawn structure, and king safety. Only then, after considering other relevant factors, both lasting and intangible, could you decide to trade or not.

As a rule, when it comes to material, winning is good, losing is bad, and trading is neither but depends on the situation at hand.

fighting for the run-down d4. It's going to need a vitamin shot against Black's invading knight.

12.   ...   Nd4

Here it is. Black's knight radiantly occupies d4. If required, the knight can be reinforced by the advance c7-c5. When doubly guarded by two pawns, and no enemy pawn can attack it, a knight is sufficiently protected to remain where it is without threat of material loss by capture. If it were captured, it would be taken by a piece of equal or greater value, and that would be no worse than a trade.

13.   Nf2   ...

The knight is not going anywhere from here soon, though it wasn't doing much at h3. At least now, if ever the occasion becomes auspicious, Kasparov can slide his king-bishop up to h3 with protection, scaring Deep Blue's queen from the c8-h3 diagonal.

13.   ...   h6

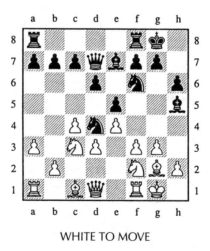

WHITE TO MOVE

Black takes steps to guard g5, preventing the dark-square bishop from attacking the f6-knight. By so hitting the knight, the bishop would also be assailing what the knight guards, the square d5. If Black's c-pawn ever goes to c5 to defend d4, White's c3-knight would love to establish residence on d5, with its view of the valley on Black's side.

The advance h7-h6 also wards off a pawn avalanche on the king's wing, which could bury Black's light-square bishop. Now, after retreating to g6, the bishop can seek refuge at h7.

But this luft-making move (a move that provides the king an escape hatch off the home rank), also furnishes White a future target, the h6-pawn.

14.   Be3   . . .

Clearing the home rank of the last queenside minor piece and threatening to capture the d4-knight. Black would then have to take back with its e-pawn, removing deterrence to f4. Eventually, so unchallenged, White's kingside pawns might push ahead, mowing down everything in their path, even light-square bishops.

14.   . . .   c5

Just in time. Black overprotects d4. If White now takes the knight, the c5-pawn can take back, enabling Black's king-pawn to stay in place as a counterpoise to White's kingside crusade.

15.   b4   b6

White tries to undermine the d4-knight's protection, and Black upholds it.

16.   Rb1   . . .

White places his rook on the b-file, in preparation of opening the file by an exchange, b4xc5.

16.   . . .   Kh8?

Huh? What's this got to do with the price of tea in China? Perhaps Deep Blue considered the plan of moving the g-pawn and didn't want its king kept on the same file. Or maybe it's just a computer thing. The machine didn't know what to do, so it made a kind of temporizing move, waiting to see if White would impair his own position. I'd like to get Kasparov's personal take on it.

Rooks, pawns, and files have an intimate relationship. From a rook's perspective (or a queen's), there are three kinds of files: a closed file, an open file, and a half-open file. A closed file contains pawns of both colors, an open file has no pawns on it at all, and a half-open file has pawns of only one color.

Neither player's rooks are able to use a closed file effectively. Either player's rooks can use an open file. And the rooks of only one player may use a half-open file (the player with no friendly pawn in the way). Thus the attacker should seek open and half-open files for his rooks (and queen). By occupying these files, his major pieces can attack the opponent's position.

If a player wants to convert a closed file into a half-open or open one so that his rooks can use it, he must rid the file of his own impeding pawn. This can be done by exchanging the pawn or by sacrificing it. In order to get the pawn into an exchangeable or sacrificeable position, the pawn should be moved up to come in contact with the opponent's pawns. Only then can it be gotten out of the way, by exchange or sacrifice, to unblock the line for major pieces.

Sometimes a rook can become active, even with a friendly pawn still in its way along the file, if that pawn is sufficiently advanced to be a menace to the opponent's community. As the pawn advances and threatens points in the enemy position, the supporting rook behind it gains in mobility and potential power. The farther up the board the pawn, the more mobile the rook. Rooks in particular are ideal for supporting the advance of passed pawns from the rear.

A passed pawn is one that is free to advance, whose movement no enemy pawn can stop by blockage or capture. It literally has passed the opponent's pawns and is able to move toward the promotion square. To stop the passed pawn, the opponent must rely on pieces, not pawns. Imagine the growing power of this monstrous pawn if supported by a rook from behind. With the rook's protection, the pawn may be able to reach the last rank to promote to a new queen.

Thus arises the useful endgame maxim: Rooks belong behind passed pawns.

It seems to me that Black's last move is reminiscent of some of those played by the primitive commercial chess-playing computers from the early eighties. Those machines, if stuck for an idea, at times would either repeat moves or play an inscrutable one.

Of course, Deep Blue is a supercomputer, programmed by a star team, holding its own against the best player in the world. It wouldn't do anything without a cogent reason. Or would it?

17.   Rb2   . . .

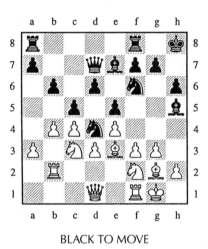

BLACK TO MOVE

It's hard to say what White should do here. He'd like to move the c3-knight to the center, but Black's f6-knight keeps d5 under observation. Meanwhile, the pin on White's f3-pawn is hampering White's efforts at a kingside attack. For now, he can't move his f-pawn. Thus Kasparov, too, plays a waiting move. It doesn't seem to do much, other than deploy the rook so that it could swerve to White's right if needed.

17.   . . .   a6

This snaillike move prepares the advance of Black's b-pawn, though it weakens b6. If White now captures the c-pawn, Black must take back with the b-pawn or lose it.

18.   bxc5   bxc5
19.   Bh3   . . .

In attempting to chase Black's queen off the c8-h3 diagonal, Kasparov offers Deep Blue a pawn sacrifice at f3. In some variations, queens are exchanged, and White enters the endgame behind by a pawn for long-term piece pressure.

For instance, if Black were now to play Bh5xf3, White keeps the heat on with 20. Bxd7 Bxd1 21. Rxd1 Nxd7 22. Rb7 Rfd8 23. Nd5. But this line is unclear, and it's up to Kasparov to increase his positional superiority.

A tactical error, however, would be 19. . . . Nxf3 + ?, which could be answered slyly by 20. Kh1!. If Black then moves its queen to safety, White wins a piece with 21. g3-g4, cutting the f3-knight's defense.

19.   ...   Qc7

Black's queen gets out of attack, so White must now save his f3-pawn.

20.   Bg4 ...

A nice idea. It secures g4, and if Black's bishop takes White's, White's f2-knight takes back, and Black's f6-knight will be captured or deflected away from the center. White's c3-knight can then move into the catbird seat at d5.

20.   ...   Bg6

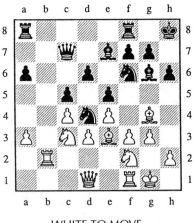

WHITE TO MOVE

Black declines the bishop trade, and now White's f-pawn is no longer pinned. It can move, and White can fuel a kingside attack.

21. f4   . . .

This threatens a further advance to f5, shutting out the g6-bishop and forcing it back to the cubbyhole at h7. If that happens, White will then withdraw the light-square bishop and push up the g-pawn. It could get ugly.

21.   . . .   exf4

This exchange copes with the problem. Since the most desirable way to take back is with the pawn, retaining fluidity in the center, White's g-pawn will no longer exist to support a pawn

---

A discovered attack is a tactic usually involving three units: two friendly ones and one of the opponent's. All three units start on the same line—the same rank, file, or diagonal.

The two friendly units consist of one that moves and one that doesn't. The one that eventually moves starts in the middle, as a temporary barrier between the enemy unit and the friendly stationary one.

When the front unit moves, it unveils a direct attack from the stationary unit on the opponent's target unit up the line. This often allows the moving unit to position itself on an otherwise endangered square with impunity, especially if the threat from the stationary unit takes precedence because it's a check. All checks must be answered, so the discovered check freezes the action, constraining the opponent to save his king.

If the moving unit also gives a threat, then the discovery is a true double attack. When both the moving and stationary unit give simultaneous check to the enemy king, it's called double check, which is one of the strongest moves in chess. The only way to get out of double check is by moving the enemy king, since it's impossible to block two checks or capture two checking units with one move.

Double check can be a devastating weapon, sometimes producing incredible checkmates. I've seen cases where the mate was so surprising, even the winner didn't realize he had won, and the loser had to point it out.

---

storm. But White gets the better game anyway, with greater flexibility and a new file to possibly use, the half-open g-file.

22.   gxf4   Qa5

It's show time. The machine resorts to its specialty, munching material. From a5, Black's queen forks a knight and a pawn, at c3 and a3 respectively. Since Kasparov is not about to retreat the threatened c3-knight to b1, just to save a measly isolated rook-pawn, he accepts the challenge, sacrificing the a-pawn for initiative and position. It's the classic matchup, material for attack, machine vs. human.

23.   Bd2   . . .

White defends his knight and creates a possible discovery. If White's c3-knight moves, his d2-bishop imperils Black's queen.

23.   . . .   Qxa3

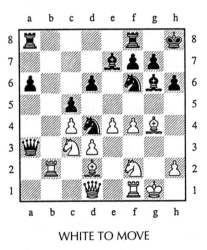

WHITE TO MOVE

An inveterate materialist, Deep Blue pounces on the a-pawn. The only question is whether it will pay for the loss of time needed to get the queen back in action. After taking the pawn, the queen is somewhat displaced, and White can swipe at it.

24.   Ra2   Qb3

Black offers to trade queens, in that it is ahead by a pawn and wants to simplify to an endgame, where it's less likely the defender will succumb to a sudden attack, especially if he is a calculating machine. Furthermore, in the endgame, material advantages tend to take on greater significance.

25. f5 Qxd1

26. Bxd1 Bh7

White pressed the kingside attack, and Black exchanged queens. Note that White recaptured the queen with the bishop to extricate it from the f6-knight's grasping sight at g4. Black then spent a tempo retreating its light-square bishop to h7.

Could Deep Blue have avoided the tomb at h7, offering a bishop trade at h5 instead? Let's see. On 26. . . . Bh5, White trades bishops, 27. Bxh5 Nxh5, and follows by centralizing the knight, 28. Nd5, which also hits the dark-square bishop.

If the bishop retreats to d8, communication between the rooks is broken, and White turns the gauge higher with Nf2-g4. If Black offers to trade the dark-square bishop instead, with 28. . . . Bg5, White is on top after trading bishops on g5 and following with Rf1-a1 or even Rf1-b1.

Clearly, it seems that the White forces have enough initiative to overcome being a pawn down, even though the queens are off the board. And with Garry Kasparov tending his own investments, White's stock is on the rise.

27. Nh3 . . .

White begins a maneuver, swerving the knight to the edge, then to f4 and d5, which is a commanding base of operations for either White knight.

Black has a few liabilities for its extra material, including an isolated pawn at a6 and a weak back pawn at d6. Moreover, both Black bishops lack scope, the dark-square bishop because of its own pawns and the light-square bishop because of the opponent's pawns. Nor are Black's rooks yet in the game. White's d3-pawn is backward, and Deep Blue has an exemplary knight at d4, but that doesn't suffice to render Black's situation enviable.

27. . . . Rfb8

A preemptive strike. Deep Blue seizes the open b-file, before White does, and activates the king-rook.

28.   Nf4   Bd8

Played to anticipate a knightly intrusion on d5, and to guard the square a5, so that the rook-pawn can be moved there with protection. Another idea was to abandon the vulnerable d5 in favor of occupying e5. This could be accomplished by retreating the f6-knight to d7, then coming back out to e5. Black's centralized knights offer compensatory activity, and White's weak d3 comes under fire.

29.   Nfd5   Nc6

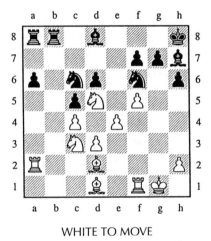

WHITE TO MOVE

White finally occupies d5, the machine ignores it, repositioning one of its own knights to sling arrows toward White's Achilles's Heel at d3. Meanwhile, if White's knight takes Black's on f6, the d8-bishop recaptures, appropriating a splendid diagonal. Since the knight was well situated at d4, withdrawing it to c6 must have been a hard decision, though not necessarily for a Machiavellian machine.

30.   Bf4   . . .

Black possesses a weak d-pawn, too, so White fastens his designs on it. And if the c6-knight moves into e5, White has the option of capturing it.

30. ... Ne5

Black targets d3, but its knight can't capture on that square without exposing the d6-pawn to seizure by the f4-bishop. To uphold d3, Kasparov could take the e5-knight, but that would cede the two bishops and actually alleviate Black's weak d6, bringing it to the more guardable e5.

31. Ba4 ...

Clearing the home rank and commandeering the a4-e8 diagonal. The d3-pawn need not be directly protected, for, if taken, White obtains a more sabotaging capture at d6.

31. ... Nxd5

32. Nxd5

White retakes with a knight to keep d5 open to pieces and further use. Recapturing with a pawn would be a serious positional mistake, forever after denying Kasparov the opportunity to capitalize by occupying his strong point.

32. ... a5

Black insures the safety of its a-pawn, but places another pawn on a dark square, further reducing the d8-bishop's scope. The advance a6-a5 also weakens b5, since it can no longer be guarded by a Black pawn.

33. Bb5 ...

White entrenches the bishop on a strong square and closes off the b-file to Black's rook. Black's retaliatory attack is nipped in the bud.

33. ... Ra7

With this, Black secures its second rank and removes the rook from a light square, so the b5-bishop can never disturb it. On the other hand, on a7, the rook doesn't have a rosy future.

34. Kg2 ...

White readies the king for endgame activity, while guarding f3, so as not to be bothered by a knight check.

34. ... g5

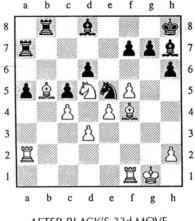

AFTER BLACK'S 33d MOVE

To get some play, Deep Blue strikes out with this precarious pawn advance, which weakens f6 and spurs White to take the knight.

35.   Bxe5 + dxe5

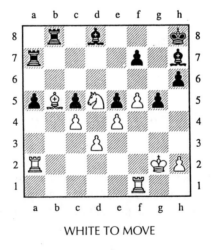

WHITE TO MOVE

White no longer has a target at d6, nor does he have two bishops. Black does, but they're not very effective. If given the chance, Black will now play f7-f6, offering its light-square bishop a way to flourish again, this time at g8. Alas, Kasparov prevents that with a small pawn push, keeping Black cramped.

36. f6!   Bg6

Black finds some fun for the light-square bishop after all. Maybe now it can reemerge at h5 and then g4.

37. h4!   ...

The mechanistic one must step carefully. If 37. . . . . Bh5, White takes the g-pawn, h4xg5; and if Black recaptures, h6xg5, White's rook pins and wins the bishop by moving to h1. Meanwhile, White threatens to take on g5 anyway, opening the h-file against Deep Blue's king.

37. ...   gxh4

White will be able to regain this pawn, but at least the IBM wonder retains some shelter for its monarch in the form of the h6-pawn.

38. Kh3   ...

White's king himself does the job. Kasparov, a great endgame player, and one of the most successful world champions of all time, understands the import of utilizing the king in the final phase.

38. ...   Kg8

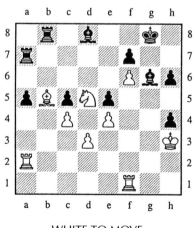

WHITE TO MOVE

Up a pawn or not, Deep Blue recognizes that the real winning chances lie with White. It therefore decides to batten down the hatches, holding the fort against a siege. It will keep the game closed. And it doesn't want to provide White with any fresh points of attack, so it bides its time, at least for now, saying, in effect, "Do me something."

39. Kxh4 . . .

White's king comes right up to the fourth rank, something inconceivable in the earlier stages. But it can go no farther, for Black's bishop and h6-pawn guard the three kingside entry squares at f5, g5, and h5.

39. . . . Kh7

40. Kg4 Bc7

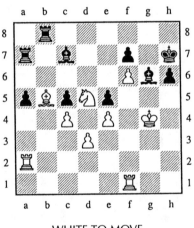

WHITE TO MOVE

White and Black jockey king moves, then suddenly Black makes a major decision. Trying to get the dark-square bishop to a possibly more effective square at d6, the machinating one places the bishop on a square where it can be taken. A pawn will be sacrificed in the bargain (the a5-pawn), an action Deep Blue never undertakes lightly, but Kasparov as White must exchange away his powerful knight in the process. That's an impressive decision, the kind of thing a sentient human might do.

41.	Nxc7	Rxc7
42.	Rxa5	...

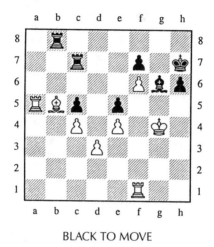

BLACK TO MOVE

Once again, it's all even, though White still retains a playing edge. Black's bishop lacks scope, and its position doesn't seem to be impregnable. White himself has one big problem, his backward d-pawn. By pressuring the pawn at d3, Deep Blue dissuades White from taking any further risks and the game is drawn.

42.	...	Rd8

This is the move that caps it. White will be tied down to defending d3, and that's that.

43.	Rf3	Kh8
44.	Kh4	Kg8

White doesn't know what to do, and Black doesn't have to do anything.

45.	Ra3	Kh8
46.	Ra6	Kh7
47.	Ra3	Kh8
48.	Ra6	Draw ($^1/_2$–$^1/_2$)

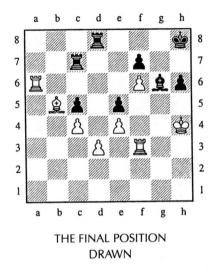

THE FINAL POSITION
DRAWN

Kasparov proposed the draw, realizing that continuing was futile, and Deep Blue's programmers and chess analysts accepted. Considering that Deep Blue had Black and was outplayed throughout most of the game, the result was quite favorable.

We're halfway through the match, and the score stands even, with one win, one loss, and one draw for each side. In chess scoring, you get a point for a win, nothing for a loss, and each side gets half a point for a draw.

The match is tied 1.5–1.5.

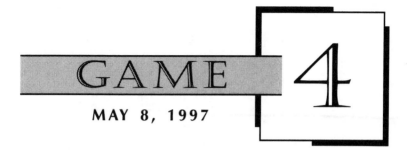

GAME 4

MAY 8, 1997

WHITE: **Deep Blue**

BLACK: **Garry Kasparov**

OPENING: **Pribyl Defense**

ECO CODE: **B07**

RESULT: **Draw in 56 moves**

SCORE: **Kasparov 2—Deep Blue 2**

THE MOVES

NO.	WHITE	BLACK	NO.	WHITE	BLACK
1.	e4	c6	29.	Rd1	Kc7
2.	d4	d6	30.	Ka1	Qxe3
3.	Nf3	Nf6	31.	fxe3	Rf7
4.	Nc3	Bg4	32.	Rh3	Ref8
5.	h3	Bh5	33.	Nd4	Rf2
6.	Bd3	e6	34.	Rb1	Rg2
7.	Qe2	d5	35.	Nce2	Rxg4
8.	Bg5	Be7	36.	Nxe6 +	Nxe6
9.	e5	Nfd7	37.	Nd4	Nxd4
10.	Bxe7	Qxe7	38.	exd4	Rxd4
11.	g4	Bg6	39.	Rg1	Rc4
12.	Bxg6	hxg6	40.	Rxg6	Rxc2
13.	h4	Na6	41.	Rxg7 +	Kb6
14.	0-0-0	0-0-0	42.	Rb3 +	Kc5
15.	Rdg1	Nc7	43.	Rxa7	Rf1 +
16.	Kb1	f6	44.	Rb1	Rff2
17.	exf6	Qxf6	45.	Rb4	Rc1 +
18.	Rg3	Rde8	46.	Rb1	Rcc2
19.	Re1	Rhf8	47.	Rb4	Rc1 +
20.	Nd1	e5	48.	Rb1	Rxb1 +
21.	dxe5	Qf4	49.	Kxb1	Re2
22.	a3	Ne6	50.	Re7	Rh2
23.	Nc3	Ndc5	51.	Rh7	Kc4
24.	b4	Nd7	52.	Rc7	c5
25.	Qd3	Qf7	53.	e6	Rxh4
26.	b5	Ndc5	54.	e7	Re4
27.	Qe3	Qf4	55.	a4	Kb3
28.	bxc6	bxc6	56.	Kc1	Draw
					(½–½)

DRAWING POWER

Once again, Deep Blue began by moving its king-pawn two squares, but instead of countering with the same move, as he did in Game 2, this time Kasparov essayed the Pribyl Defense. By move 6 Garry had advanced three middle pawns only one square each, assuming a crouching but flexible position.

A critical juncture occurred at move 11, when the machine weakened its kingside pawn structure just to inflict doubled pawns. After castling queenside, Black broke open the king-bishop file, turning his weaknesses into strengths. In particular, he attacked along the open lines concurrent with the doubled pawns.

Patrolling the e- and f-files with major pieces, Kasparov constrained Deep Blue to deploy a rook awkwardly, just to keep the position together. So that his pieces would flourish more, Kasparov then sacrificed a pawn, and as the champ's knights secured power bases, the machine clung to its material for dear existence.

Seeking to cash in on a favorable endgame, even though a pawn down, Kasparov traded queens. This left White's pawn structure in tatters. But Deep Blue rose to the challenge. Intuitively, it seemed, for the variations were unclear, the machine gave back its extra pawn to obtain a freer game.

Here Kasparov perhaps erred. He chose to accept the pawn gift, which liberated White's immured rook. Black still pressed his onslaught, but again, the machine proved resilient, manufacturing a mating net out of thin air. Kasparov averted the mate, traded a pair of rooks, and though he mobilized a couple of dangerous passed pawns, Deep Blue found enough counterplay to hold the champ at bay. Clearly, neither player could force a win, and the game was drawn by agreement.

White		**Black**
Deep Blue		Garry Kasparov

1.	e4	c6
2.	d4	d6
3.	Nf3	Nf6
4.	Nc3	Bg4

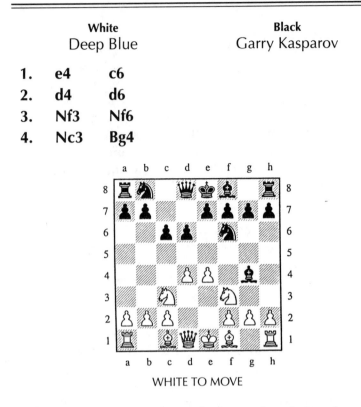

WHITE TO MOVE

Kasparov is using an unusual move order, designed to take Deep Blue out of its opening library. He's combined elements of three opening systems: the Caro-Kann Defense, the Pirc Defense, and Tartakover's Old Indian Defense. In another few moves, he'll push the king-pawn up one square, e7-e6, followed by d6-d5, adding a French Defense tinge to the cocktail.

How is Deep Blue coping with all of this? Internally, the computer is searching its transpositional tables, hoping to come across something recognizable. On the board, Deep Blue is making reasonable moves, controlling center squares and developing its pieces.

5.   h3   . . .

Posing a question: is Black going to take the knight or withdraw the bishop?

> *A typical dilemma is what to do when you have a knight on a bishop-three square (for White, c3 or f3; for Black, c6 or f6) and your opponent's bishop pins or attacks it by moving to a knight-five square (Bb5 or Bg5, for a White bishop to attack a Black knight; or Bb4 or Bg4, for a Black bishop to attack a White knight).*
>
> *You can force your opponent to declare his intentions by "putting the question to the bishop." This you do by attacking the bishop with a rook-pawn, advancing either a2-a3, or h2-h3, for a White pawn to attack a Black bishop on b4 or g4 respectively; or a7-a6, or h7-h6, for a Black pawn to attack a White bishop on b5 or g5. Once the bishop is threatened by the pawn, it will have to take the knight or retreat to safety.*
>
> *If the stratagem works, it will free you up to pursue other plans. If it fails, it might leave you with weaknesses, without achieving freedom or clarity. In some cases, it may even backfire if the enemy has other pieces in the region. So put the question to the bishop, but make sure you know the answer and like it ahead of time.*

5.   . . .   Bh5

Kasparov maintains the tension by retreating the bishop, hoping to provoke the steel wonder into breaking the pin completely with g2-g4.

6.   Bd3   e6
7.   Qe2   . . .

White's last two moves develop and reinforce the king-pawn.

7.   . . .   d5

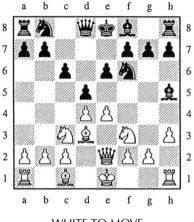

WHITE TO MOVE

Starting here, the game acquires its own character, and the play really begins. The advance of Kasparov's d-pawn creates tension in the center, and along with the tension is a threat to win White's d4-pawn by 8. . . . dxe4 9. Nxe4 Bxf3 10. Qxf3 Qxd4.

8. Bg5   . . .

Deep Blue counters by attacking the f6-point. The attempt to win the d4-pawn by 8. . . . dxe4 9. Nxe4 Bxf3 10. Qxf3 Qxd4? would explode in Black's own hands after 11. Nxf6+ gxf6 12. Bxf6, forking queen and rook.

8. . . .   Be7

Deep Blue's last move also contained the threat of e4-e5, piling up on the pinned f6-knight. With this quiet building move of the bishop, Kasparov breaks the pin and renews the threat of d5xe4, uncovering the queen's assault on d4.

9. e5   . . .

There were two ways to end the central tension. White could exchange at d5, or advance his e4-pawn. Exchanging 9. exd5 leaves Black with an easy game after 9. . . . cxd5. So Deep Blue advances, picking up central space and going at the f6-knight.

9. ... Nfd7

The knight withdraws, out of harm's way, at the same time unmasking an attack on the g5-bishop.

10. Bxe7 ...

Deep Blue prefers not to lose time retreating the bishop. So an exchange takes place on e7.

Often you can gain time by exchanging off a threatened piece. The point is that your opponent will have to expend a tempo to take back. You will then get the next free move. If you retreat your menaced piece to safety instead, unless you can do so with a threat, your opponent gets the next unfettered move.

Exchanging can lose time in several ways. If your opponent can take back and assemble his forces with threats and more energy, you will probably lose the initiative.

You might also lose time if you solve your opponent's problems for him, trading off a good piece for a bad one (one that's not too active). In that event, you may be able to save time later by wasting time now. Simply retreat your threatened piece out of attack, for then your opponent might still have to spend a few moves improving his inactive piece.

10. ... Qxe7

On the surface, a simple recapture. But there's a threat involved. Black is hoping to take the knight, Bh5xf3, and after White takes back, Qe2xf3, fork two pawns, at b2 and d4, by invading with the queen to b4. This prompts Deep Blue to chase the Black bishop off the d1-h5 diagonal, so that the f3-knight cannot be captured at all.

11. g4 Bg6

And now an exchange of light-square bishops has become inevitable. The trade could very well take place on d3, but Deep Blue is anxious to inflict doubled pawns.

12. Bxg6 hxg6

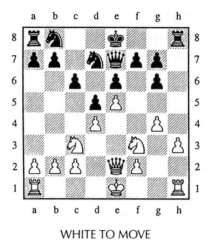

WHITE TO MOVE

The natural recapture, toward the center, just as they recommend in the books. At one stroke, without even having to move, the h8-rook becomes enterprising on the open file.

Technically, you could also make a case for 12. . . . fxg6, capturing away from the center, with subsequent play on the f-file. But Kasparov rejects this approach as too one-dimensional. He wants his f-pawn kept intact, on the f-file. In this way, he can still attack White's center by f7-f6.

13.   h4   . . .

Deep Blue takes time out to place its h-pawn on a square where it can be defended by his f3-knight. This relieves the h1-rook for subsequent action. There is also the thought that if Black castles kingside, White can charge ahead with the h-pawn, fueling the fire around Black's king.

13.   . . .   Na6

Naturally, Kasparov has no intention of placing his king under the gun by kingside castling. With the text move he prepares to evacuate his queen to the queenside.

14.   0-0-0   0-0-0

Both sides have the same idea, to castle queenside. On the

queen's wing it seems the kings are safe, for now, and play can proceed on the opposite flank.

> *No matter where the queens and kings wind up, the queenside consists of thirty-two squares, including all those on the a-, b-, c-, and d-files. The kingside is the board's other half, which is made up of all the squares on the e-, f-, g-, and h-files.*

15.   Rdg1   . . .

Deep Blue is still looking to advance the h-pawn: 16. h5 gxh5 17. gxh5, with vertical pressure on the g7-pawn.

15.   . . .   Nc7

Kasparov is not concerned about Deep Blue's "threat" and brings his knight on the edge back into society. In the event of 16. h5, Kasparov is not obliged to capture. He can sidestep with 16. . . . g5 17. Qe3 f6, and everything is copacetic.

16.   Kb1   . . .

Unable to see any way into Black's camp, Deep Blue follows its programming, passing with a king move. It's up to Kasparov to initiate the action.

16.   . . .   f6

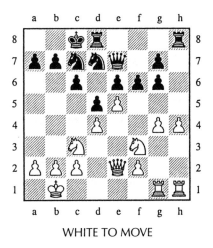

WHITE TO MOVE

And Kasparov is quick to respond. He refrains from c6-c5, as that would entail moving a pawn in front of his king, with attendant weakening of the castled position.

In this game, at least, Kasparov has programmed himself not to allow Deep Blue even the slightest look-in at his king.

With 16. . . . f7-f6, Kasparov begins the process of trying to break down the wall of White pawns in the center. In addition, there is also the prospect of opening the f-file for his rooks.

17.   exf6   . . .

White has to head off the capture 17. . . . fxe5, when the recapture 18. dxe5 would result in e5 becoming a dead square for the White pieces. Ideally, White would like to take back with its f3-knight, but can't. After 18. Nxe5 Nxe5 19. Qxe5, Black picks up the insufficiently defended rook-pawn by 19. . . . Rxh4.

The only way out is to capture the Black f6-pawn first.

17.   . . .   Qxf6!

And not 17. . . . gxf6?, for White could then gain piece control of e5 by 18. g5! f5 19. Ne5 Nxe5 20. Qxe5. In that case, with Black having no pawn to guard them, the dark center squares are firmly in White's grasp. The pressure could be increased by the knight artifice, 20. Nc3-e2 and 21. Ne2-f4.

Kasparov's recapture with the queen insures counterplay on the newly open f-file. At the same time, the pressure exerted by the queen and h8-rook on White's h4-pawn prevents the f3-knight from jumping into e5.

18.   Rg3   . . .

Deep Blue goes over to defense. A Black rook will shortly appear at f8, so White overprotects its f3-knight in anticipation.

18.   . . .   Rde8

A reminder to White that if it relaxes its hold on e5, the Black e6-pawn is ready to step up.

19.   Re1   . . .

Deep Blue abandons any further thoughts of advancing its h-pawn. The rook transfers to the e-file in order to keep watch over the central e5-point.

19. ... Rhf8

As expected, a Kasparov rook moves over to the f-file.

20. Nd1 ...

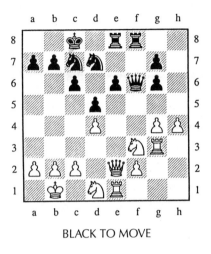

BLACK TO MOVE

An amazing move. The knight retreats to an obviously awkward and seemingly pointless square. But there's a method behind Deep Blue's apparent madness.

The f2-pawn is protected and the f3-knight is now ready to spring to e5. For example: 21. Ne5 Nxe5 22. Qxe5 Qxe5 23. Rxe5, and, lo and behold, White has established a dark-square bind. And once Deep Blue gets to this position, it shouldn't be difficult to unearth the threefold plan f2-f3, Nd1-f2, and Nf2-d3, and augmenting the bind.

Clearly, Kasparov must find something, and he has to find it fast.

20. ... e5!

Find a dagger move like this, and you'll short-circuit anyone's game.

White's knight cannot very well come to e5. If 21. Nxe5 Nxe5 22. dxe5 Qxh4, White's kingside starts leaking like a sieve. And since Black's e5-pawn has to be taken, else it steamrolls onward, there's only one way to do it. With the queen-pawn.

21.   dxe5   . . .

White has an extra pawn, but also that dead spot at e5. That
dead spot means the machine can't make its pieces gel. They
just stand around, inanimate, discombobulated, unable to coor-
dinate with one another.

Kasparov's forces, on the other hand, work together nicely.
He easily dodges the White e5-pawn without discomfort. The
knights can make use of the blockading square e6, and the heavy
pieces continually threaten invasion down the f-file.

That's what a good positional pawn sac will do for your
game, and there's no one better at this ploy than Garry Kasparov.

21.   . . .   Qf4
22.   a3   . . .

This looks like another computer pass. There is no necessity
to guard the square b4 at this moment. Maybe Deep Blue is making an airhole for its king to avoid a back-rank mate one day, in
the merry, merry month of May.

22.   . . .   Ne6
23.   Nc3   . . .

Both sides ameliorate the position of their knights. But further
improvement for White is rather difficult, the machine's pieces
being confined to the trenches of the first three ranks.

23.   . . .   Ndc5

Here the Black knight acts as an agent provocateur. It's as
though Kasparov has already divined Deep Blue's response.

24.   b4   . . .

And Deep Blue rises to the bait. The c5-knight is chased
back, but at the same time, White has weakened the structure in
front of its castled king. Computers are prone to play moves like
this because they calculate everything. Humans are more likely
to filter out risky pawn moves from their thoughts. Okay, not all
humans . . .

24.   . . .   Nd7

The knight coils back to d7, ready to spring anew to b6 and
c4.

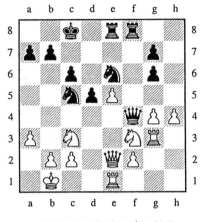

AFTER BLACK'S 23d MOVE

25. Qd3 ...

Another attack, this time on the g6-pawn, sends Kasparov's queen into retreat.

25. ... Qf7

26. b5 ...

Deep Blue continues the forward motion, unconcerned about the safety of the White king. The idea is to get at Kasparov's king by 27. bxc6 bxc6 28. Qa6 +.

26. ... Ndc5

But now it's Kasparov's turn. And the knight reemerges, pushing Deep Blue's queen off the a6-f1 diagonal.

27. Qe3 Qf4

And the Black queen also materializes. It's clear that Deep Blue's initiative was purely temporary. Kasparov's queen and knight are back on their old stands, stronger than ever. But at least Deep Blue gets to punch a few holes in Kasparov's position.

28. bxc6 bxc6

29. Rd1 ...

The rook has nothing more to do on the e-file, so it shifts to

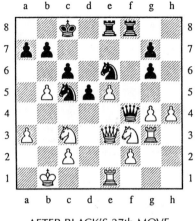

AFTER BLACK'S 27th MOVE

the d-file, where it keeps the d4-square under close observation, just like its master.

29. ... Kc7

A little housekeeping move. The king steps up a square, giving protection to the undefended c6-pawn. At the same time, the b8-square is vacated for possible use by a Black rook, coming over to harass White's king.

30. Ka1 ...

A precautionary move. Deep Blue cannot stop a Black rook from shifting to b8, but at least the machine's king can seek shelter from the coming storm.

30. ... Qxe3

Kasparov chooses the safest continuation. He trades queens, doubles White's e-pawns, and looks forward to penetrating White's position via the f-file. In short, Kasparov is endeavoring to win in the endgame.

The alternative was to keep queens on the board for the purpose of trying to get at Deep Blue's king. But it's not so easy to arrange.

For example, if 30. . . . Qc4, there could follow 31. Nd4 Rf4 (trying to transfer heavy pieces along the fourth rank runs into

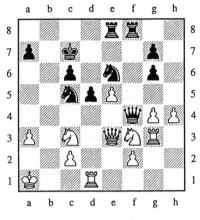

AFTER WHITE'S 30th MOVE

trouble) 32. Nxe6 + Rxe6 33. Rxd5! cxd5 34. Qxf4! Qxf4 35. Nxd5 + (welcome to fork city) and 36. Nxf4.

31.   fxe3   . . .

The White pawns are a horrible mess. They're doubled, they're isolated, and they're scattered over four different pawn islands.

Still, there is no clear way to get at them. A frontal assault by 31. . . . Nd7 and 32. . . . Nec5 is not convincing. As soon as the Black knight leaves c5, White breaks out with the advance e3-e4.

The only sure way to get at the weak White pawns is from the rear. Double rooks on the f-file penetrate to the opponent's second rank and envelop the pawns from behind. That's the Kasparov plan.

31.   . . .   Rf7

The first step is to double the rooks.

32.   Rh3   . . .

Computer passes. There's not much else to do. Let's go see the show.

32.   . . .   Ref8

Black completes the doubling process, threatening to capture the f3-knight.

A mighty assault weapon is a battery of two rooks, or "doubled rooks." When lined up along the same rank or file, with nothing in between, the rooks are twice as strong in that the back one reinforces the front one for attack or defense. If the front rook is taken, its associate can take back.

---

33.   Nd4   . . .

The knight gives way, opening a path for the rooks to enter. The attempt to make a stand on the f-file by 33. Rf1 is doomed to failure. White ends up in a terrible self-pin, while Black can make continued inroads, pushing the d-pawn or invading on e4 with the knight.

33.   . . .   Rf2

Kasparov follows through with the plan he has mapped out for himself, with the rook entering White's second rank. An alternative approach was to first exchange knights by 33. . . . Nxd4 34. exd4 Ne6. Here the attack on the d4-pawn ties down the d1-rook to its defense. And White still has no way of preventing Black's rook from invading on f2, or other rook entries for that matter.

34.   Rb1!   . . .

Very sly for a chunk of metal. Kasparov has his open f-file, so Deep Blue wants an open file of her own. (I think it's female.)

At first glance, placing the White rook at b1 looks rather pointless, since the Black king stands guard over the invasion squares b8 and b7. But lying just under the surface are certain tactical details that will allow the b1-rook to penetrate, should Kasparov become careless.

34.   . . .   Rg2!

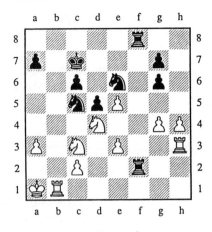

AFTER WHITE'S 34th MOVE

Kasparov is in for the kill. Veering the rook over to the g-file, he swats at the vulnerable g4-pawn, while preparing entry for the f8-colleague to join the party at f2.

35.　Nce2　...

It's not worth taking time out to save the sickly g4-pawn by 35. g5. Kasparov would immediately launch his other rook onto the second rank, 35. . . . Rff2, and White could hardly find a useful move.

The difference in the strength of the rooks is patently obvious. Black's rooks are working at full power, while the White rooks stand by as helpless observers.

Therefore, Deep Blue, with the text (Nc3-e2), begins a new line of defense. Not stopping to count pawns, White's idea is to trade off all the knights, and in so doing, obtain freedom for its rooks to become active.

35.　...　Rxg4

At this point, Kasparov is faced with one of those typical decisions that every chess player encounters. Do you increase the pressure on the enemy position, or do you cash in and take the greenbacks while you can? After being down a pawn for so long, it's understandable that he opts to capture the g-pawn and re-store material equality. Especially so, since he still retains the better chances.

So he could just as easily have continued with 35. . . . Rff2, piling on the seventh-rank power, letting the g-pawn go until later.

36.   Nxe6 + Nxe6

37.   Nd4   Nxd4

In his desire to become a player of chessic means, Black per-haps commits a mistake. This exchange allows White's third-rank rook to finally join the party. Instead of playing to win a pawn by trading knights on d4, Kasparov might have tried mov-ing the knight to c5, keeping a grip on e4.

38.   exd4   Rxd4

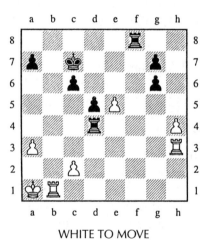

WHITE TO MOVE

This is the position that arose on Deep Blue's internal elec-tronic chessboard. Yes, that's right, computers are allowed to move the pieces around while the game is still in progress. For humans, that's a no-no.

Outwardly, there does not look to be anything particularly attractive about White's position. True, the knights have been vaporized off the board, and the rooks are free to roam, but the pawn count is five to four, in GK's favor.

39.   Rg1   ...

The inexorable mashing of moves that takes place in Deep Blue's interior has unearthed a clear-cut line of play that will shift the balance of pawns in White's favor. One by one by one, three Kasparov pawns drop off the board.

39.   ...   Rc4

There's no way to hold the anemic g6-pawn. Best to go after the c2-pawn and reestablish pressure on the second rank.

40.   Rxg6   Rxc2

41.   Rxg7 +   Kb6

42.   Rb3 +   ...

After a long period of inactivity, both White rooks are starting to pull their weight. Now escaping with the king to a5 is inadvisable in that a rook mate follows at a7. But moving the king to a6 isn't recommendable either, for it winds up trapped on the a-file, cut off by the rook at b3. So, like it or not, Kasparov has to let the third pawn go. Bye-bye a7-pawn.

42.   ...   Kc5

43.   Rxa7   ...

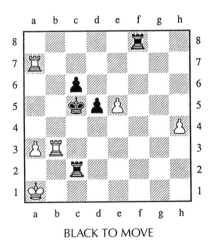

BLACK TO MOVE

Time to do the standard computer computation. Count the pawns: three to two in White's favor. You'll never be a good computer, or a good chess player, if you don't know how to add.

The quantity of pawns, however, is not the only factor in the equation. The quality of the pawns also needs to be registered. And here we must figure in Kasparov's two connected passed pawns. They are more formidable as a unit than White's three pawns, which are isolated and dispersed.

Factor in the activity of the rooks, plus the relative safety of the kings and you still get Black holding the advantage. But is it enough to win?

43.   ...   Rf1 +

This move looks awfully strong. The rook interjects itself into the proceedings with check and consequent gain of time. And yet doubts remain. Because somehow Deep Blue is able to wiggle and squirm and ultimately elude the Kasparov clutch.

44.   Rb1   Rff2

Black's doubled rooks on the seventh rank threaten a mate in one move at a2. White has to move its b1-rook in order to give its king some breathing room.

45.   Rb4!   ...

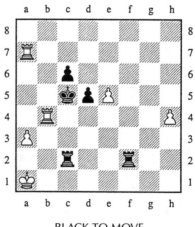

BLACK TO MOVE

Staggering! Out of nowhere, the inhuman beast has conjured up its own mate in one threat: 46. Ra5#. Kasparov's victory celebration goes on hold. Black has to play with circumspection. He's got his own king to worry about.

First a series of repetitions so Kasparov can regain his equilibrium.

45.	**. . .**	**Rc1 +**
46.	**Rb1**	**Rcc2**
47.	**Rb4**	**Rc1 +**

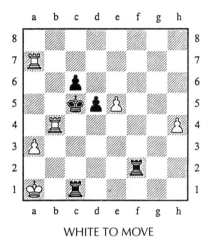

WHITE TO MOVE

As the shock effect of Deep Blue's 45th move wears off, Kasparov sees that 47. . . . . Ra2 + is insufficient for success. For example: 48. Kb1 Rxa3 (removing the protection for the b4-rook) 49. Rxa3 Kxb4 50. Rh3! (getting behind the passed pawn, while maintaining a third-rank cutoff) Re2 51. h5 Rxe5 52. h6 Re8 53. h7 Rh8 54. Kc2, and Black cannot make progress with his rook trapped in the corner.

48.	**Rb1**	**Rxb1 +**

One more repetition and the same position will have recurred three times, enabling Deep Blue's team to claim a draw. It's a rule.

A game can be drawn by threefold repetition when the same position occurs for the third time. The repetitions do not have to take place on consecutive moves, and the draw must be announced by the player before he actually plays the third repetition, not afterward. If he plays the move and then declares his intention to draw, he loses the right to claim a draw until the next occurrence.

The concept of repetition refers not to a particular move, but to an entire position. In each of the recurrences, every piece and pawn must be on the same squares and they must have the same powers in each of the repetitions.

For instance, if both a king and rook are on their original squares in two apparent repetitions, but in the first case castling is possible, and in the second case castling is impossible, the two positions are not true repetitions.

Usually, it's the inferior side that seeks a draw by threefold repetition as a way to avert potential defeat. Since the repetitions do not have to happen on consecutive moves, it's quite possible that in complex situations the player with the advantage might accidentally stumble repeatedly into the same position and allow a draw.

In his 1971 candidates match with Tigran Petrosian, on the road to his world-championship victory over Boris Spassky, Bobby Fischer salvaged a key half point by picking up on his opponent's vacillations to claim such a draw just before Petrosian enabled Fischer to repeat the position for a third time.

With the exchange of rooks, Kasparov signals his intention to keep the game going. But his energy level is running down, and so too is the energy level of the position. Each exchange drains off more juice from the board.

49.   Kxb1   Re2

An attack on the undefended e-pawn. DB places it under the rook's protection.

50.   Re7   . . .
50.   . . .   Rh2

And now an attack on the loose h-pawn, which is promptly placed under a rook's watchful eye.

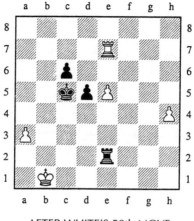

AFTER WHITE'S 50th MOVE

The girls and boys in the inquest room thought that 50. . . . d4 provided more winning chances. But it should come to the same thing that actually transpired. In fact, Deep Blue's defense would be almost exactly the same as in the game.

First, the h-pawn advances just enough to distract Black's rook: 51. h5 Rh2.

Second, the e-pawn moves up in order to tie the Black rook to the e-file: 52. Rd7 Rxh5 53. e6 Re5 54. e7 Kc4.

Third, White's king inches closer to the potential queening squares: 55. Kc2 Re2+ 56. Kd1 d3.

Fourth, White's rook harasses the c-pawn, tying Black's king close to defense: 57. Rc7 c5.

And finally, White calls on its passed a-pawn to distract the Black king from the defense of the c-pawn: 58. a4.

And the game has to end in a draw, barring of course, blunders from either side. Can machines and/or world champions blunder?

51.   Rh7   Kc4

If you thought GK was just putzing around with his last two moves, you're mistaken. Garry Klever was setting the final pitfall for the azure monster to fall into: 52. e6 c5 53. e7 Re2, and

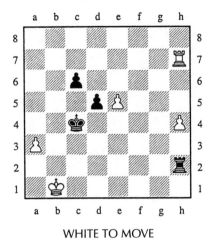

WHITE TO MOVE

suddenly White's rook is trapped on the wrong side of its e-pawn.

However, Deep Blue is up to the task.

52.   Rc7!   c5

53.   e6!   . . .

The h-pawn has served its purpose and can be abandoned.

53.   . . .   Rxh4

54.   e7   Re4

We're still following a scenario similar to the one outlined in the analytical note to move fifty. The game is drawing to a close.

55.   a4   Kb3

A final joke. Another mate-in-one threat: 56. . . . Re1#.
Deep Blue coldly slips away.

56.   Kc1   . . .

And Kasparov proposed a draw, which was accepted by Deep Blue and its attendants (the latter actually get to make this decision).

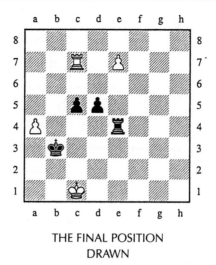

THE FINAL POSITION
DRAWN

After 56. . . . Kxa4 57. Rxc5 Rxe7 58. Rxd5, there's nothing left but skin and bones.

If Kasparov wanted to be melodramatic, he could have tried: 56. . . . c4 57. a5 c3 58. Kd1 d4 59. a6 d3 60. a7 d2, but the result would be the same after 61. Rb7+ Kc4 62. Rc7+ Kb3, with a draw by perpetual check or repetition of position.

In any case, Black cannot afford 62. . . . Kd3?, which loses to 64. Rd7+ Kc4 65. Rxd2!. Black's threats evaporate, and White queens its a-pawn.

A tough game. Kasparov was very close to winning, but in the hand-to-hand fighting, Deep Blue came away unscathed.

The match is tied 2–2.

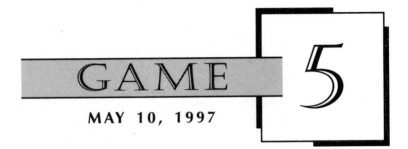

GAME 5

MAY 10, 1997

WHITE: **Garry Kasparov**

BLACK: **Deep Blue**

OPENING: **Reti Opening/King's Indian Attack**

ECO CODE: **A07**

RESULT: **Draw in 49 moves**

SCORE: **Kasparov 2.5—Deep Blue 2.5**

THE MOVES

NO.	WHITE	BLACK	NO.	WHITE	BLACK
1.	Nf3	d5	26.	Qa4	Rd8
2.	g3	Bg4	27.	Re1	Nb6
3.	Bg2	Nd7	28.	Qc2	Qd6
4.	h3	Bxf3	29.	c4	Qg6
5.	Bxf3	c6	30.	Qxg6	fxg6
6.	d3	e6	31.	b3	Nxf2
7.	e4	Ne5	32.	Re6	Kc7
8.	Bg2	dxe4	33.	Rxg6	Rd7
9.	Bxe4	Nf6	34.	Nh4	Nc8
10.	Bg2	Bb4+	35.	Bd5	Nd6
11.	Nd2	h5	36.	Re6	Nb5
12.	Qe2	Qc7	37.	cxb5	Rxd5
13.	c3	Be7	38.	Rg6	Rd7
14.	d4	Ng6	39.	Nf5	Ne4
15.	h4	e5	40.	Nxg7	Rd1+
16.	Nf3	exd4	41.	Kc2	Rd2+
17.	Nxd4	0-0-0	42.	Kc1	Rxa2
18.	Bg5	Ng4	43.	Nxh5	Nd2
19.	0-0-0	Rhe8	44.	Nf4	Nxb3+
20.	Qc2	Kb8	45.	Kb1	Rd2
21.	Kb1	Bxg5	46.	Re6	c4
22.	hxg5	N6e5	47.	Re3	Kb6
23.	Rhe1	c5	48.	g6	Kxb5
24.	Nf3	Rxd1+	49.	g7	Kb4
25.	Rxd1	Nc4		Draw (½–½)	

MECHANICAL DRAW

The opening starts the same as in Game 1, but early on, Deep Blue varies and winds up surrendering a bishop for a knight, signaling a change in its program. It doesn't necessarily imbue bishops with more value than knights anymore.

Again Kasparov plays anomalous moves to obscure the right schemes. Deep Blue can calculate fifteen plays ahead (eight moves for itself, seven for its opponent), if the play is tactical and clear. But there's still some question about its ability to wend its way through the strategic forest when there's nothing definite on the horizon.

To this end, Kasparov willingly moves his king-bishop several times to avoid trading pieces, and gradually the position emerges in his favor, as both players castle queenside as they did in the previous game.

This time, however, it's Deep Blue which offers a pawn for activity, but Kasparov continues unabated in his battle to dominate. He declines the pawn and dominates the center for constant pressure. Although Deep Blue defends clumsily, it tactically stays in there, until the fateful determination to trade queens in a way that accepts a debilitating doubled pawn.

Kasparov seizes this sudden opportunity, breaking through on the kingside to create a dangerous passed pawn, which he proceeds to escort toward the promotion square on g8. In a position that many players would have abandoned as hopeless, Deep Blue finds an ingenious saving idea, which seems to go nowhere until everyone, perhaps even Kasparov, is hit with a realization that the machine has contrived a miraculous perpetual check, salvaging the draw. It's the kind of situation that only a computer would bother to look at, because it looks at everything, even the improbable. In missing this golden chance to win a game, Kasparov may have lost an entire match.

	White Garry Kasparov	Black Deep Blue

1.	Nf3	d5
2.	g3	Bg4

So far the opening moves are the same as in Game 1. There, Kasparov began a second fianchetto on the queenside with 3. b2-b3. Here, he completes the first one on the kingside. Always honor your commitments.

3.	Bg2	Nd7

Deep Blue stays with the same opening setup used in that first game. The knight goes to d7 and later the pawns will be placed at c6 and e6. Nevertheless, the machine's crew may have added a few wrinkles, as we will soon see.

4.	h3	. . .

This diminutive pawn move was also seen in that first game, but at a later stage, on move nine. In moving the rook-pawn at an earlier stage, the champ intends to check out Deep Blue's programming. He's especially curious whether an adjustment has been made. Will the bishop withdraw to h5, as it did before, or will it this time take the knight?

4.	. . .	Bxf3

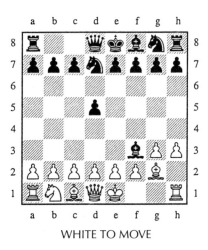

WHITE TO MOVE

There you have it. The program has been modified. The computer no longer gives undue weight to retaining the bishop. Once White has expended a tempo with his h-pawn, the trade makes good sense.

As for the so-called "superiority" of the bishop over the knight, this is more a matter of statistics rather than an inherent quality. The two pieces really are about even. It's just that the handling of the knights requires more ingenuity.

What Deep Blue doesn't grasp at the present moment is that later on, as the game webs with intricacy, it will have to play with great resourcefulness to obtain maximum performance from the knights.

5.   Bxf3   ...

The correct recapture. Taking back with the pawn would unnecessarily double White's f-pawns, closing down the g2-bishop's long diagonal.

5.   ...   c6

Deep Blue guards the d5-pawn, effectually blunting the activity of the flanked king-bishop.

6.   d3   ...

Kasparov prepares for the central thrust, e2-e4.

6.   ...   e6

A mild surprise. Most onlookers were expecting e7-e5, establishing two Black pawns in the center. But a case can also be made for the text move, which blends better with Black's remaining bishop.

It turns out, however, that Deep Blue has an ulterior motive for not placing a pawn on e5. It wants to retain that square for use by its d7-knight.

7.   e4   Ne5

This move really was astonishing. The knight attacks the bishop, which will just move away out of range for safety. White then threatens to expel the knight with consequent gain of time, soon advancing on it with either the d-pawn (d3-d4) or the f-pawn (f2-f4). Back at g2, White's bishop keeps its attacking

> *For the sake of harmony, and if it works in the situation at hand, place your pawns on squares different in color from those controlled by your bishop. This way, the bishop is not obstructed, and squares of both colors are guarded and attacked.*
>
> *Inexperienced players are often confused by this, thinking it makes more sense to place their pawns on squares of the same color so that their bishop can defend them.*
>
> *But unless there is something in a position that definitely requires this approach, playing so defensively is needless overkill. By neglecting control of the other-color squares, you offer your opponent various points of entry that at critical moments may not be defensible.*
>
> *Thus, if you have a light-square bishop, aim to place your pawns on dark squares. And if your bishop travels on dark squares, situate your pawns on light ones.*
>
> *In cases where you still retain both bishops, play flexibly, with an eye to the future. Try to determine which one of the two bishops will survive longer, or which one will be more meaningful, and position your pawns accordingly, to anticipate what may ensue.*
>
> *If your pawn position is already fixed in place, try to retain the more effective minor piece (it might not be a bishop at all), trading off the ones less able to complement the given pawn structure.*

range along the a8-h1 diagonal, while Black's knight is driven from its pedestal.

8.   Bg2   . . .

The bishop recedes to safety, still keeping an eye on the middle. Now there's an impending d3-d4 on the horizon, chasing Black's keystone knight off its imperious perch.

8.   . . .   dxe4

This exchange is meant to divert White's d-pawn off the queen-file by d3xe4. A trade of queens would ensue, with White forfeiting the right to castle. Black could then castle queenside, checking White's king, but it could find a haven at e2. White would then be threatening to gain center space by pushing pawns to f4 and e5.

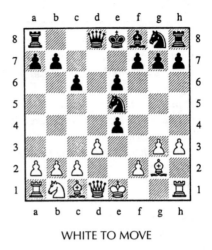

WHITE TO MOVE

9.   Bxe4   ...

Kasparov is not ready to exchange queens. He's a great end-game player, but he hasn't yet acquired a winning advantage, so why trade down?

9.   ...   Nf6

So far Deep Blue's knights are putting on a fine display. It seems that every time the machine moves a knight, Kasparov retreats the king-bishop.

There are two basic strategies in chess, to simplify or to compli-cate. If you are ahead in material, you should simplify. If you are behind, you should complicate.

You simplify by exchanging pieces and by avoiding complex, un-certain variations. Your aim should be to reduce risk. You complicate by avoiding trades, to keep as much on the board as reasonable. You should seek positions offering labyrinthine tactics and posing knotty problems.

Generally, if you are winning you want to simplify to keep control of your advantage. But if you are losing, you want to complicate to confuse your opponent. The thinking is, if losing, you have nothing to lose.

10.   Bg2   . . .

Kasparov loses a move in retreating the bishop, but he figures he can regain the tempo by advancing the d-pawn, driving back the e5-knight.

10.   . . .   Bb4 +

Harassment tactics. If White blocks the check with the c-pawn, which is the natural move in analogous cases, the e5-knight, with the Black queen's approving support, captures the pawn on d3 with check.

11.   Nd2   . . .

This avoids the possibility of doubled pawns that would stem from an exchange on c3, if the knight were placed on that square and the bishop took it, and it keeps the c-pawn unblocked so that it could advance in the future.

For the moment, it appears as if Deep Blue has thwarted the advance of Kasparov's d-pawn. But it's purely temporary. Once White castles, so that the pawn on d3 can't be taken with check, he threatens c2-c3, pushing away the b4-bishop. Then White can follow with d3-d4, driving back the e5-knight. Black needs another idea.

11.   . . .   h5!?

And here it is. If White now castles, Black intends to advance the h-pawn farther, and if White then pushes past, g3-g4, the e5-knight can drop back to g6, aiming for entry on the weakened square f4.

12.   Qe2   . . .

Kasparov postpones castling, delaying for a move to threaten the e5-knight.

12.   . . .   Qc7!

The exclamation mark is for the realization that Deep Blue has lost the initial skirmish and has made the appropriate adjustment. With the text move, Qd8-c7, Black guards its centralized knight and keeps the a3-f8 diagonal clear, in case the dark-square bishop needs to retreat.

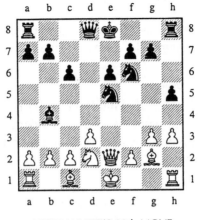

AFTER WHITE'S 12th MOVE

13.   c3   . . .

Shooing away the bishop, and adding protection to d4 so that White can then drive away the e5-knight by advancing the queen-pawn.

13.   . . .   Be7

14.   d4   Ng6

15.   h4   . . .

By blocking the h-pawn, Kasparov puts an end to Black's rook-pawn push (h5-h4) once and for all. Direct your attention to White's pawns on d4, g3, and h4. Their placement is designed to restrict the movement of the g6-knight, leaving it nothing to do.

15.   . . .   e5

Deep Blue strikes back in the center, hoping to shake the d4-pawn loose from its moorings. At stake is the freedom of the g6-knight and, possibly, the ultimate contest of human vs. machine.

16.   Nf3   exd4

The logical follow-up. Deep Blue plays to obliterate the White d4-pawn. A mistake would be the push e5-e4 instead, for after 17. Ng5, Black's king-pawn is surrounded and lost.

17.   Nxd4   . . .

The alternative recapture, 17. cxd4, is not desirable here. The isolated d4-pawn would prove vulnerable after Black castles queenside, with Black having firm control of the blockading square d5.

17.   . . .   0-0-0

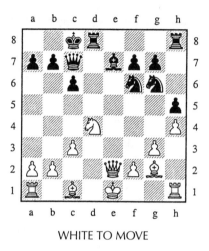

WHITE TO MOVE

Deep Blue completes the development of its forces, removing the king to safety and connecting the rooks for action.

At the moment, Kasparov has to be chary. He's a bit behind in development, and his king remains uncastled. For this reason, invading on f5 with the knight is too venturesome.

For example, if 18. Nf5, Black can offer material for attack by 18. . . . Rhe8. If White takes the trifling g-pawn, 19. Nxg7, whether bagatelle or not, he gets more than he bargained for by 19. . . . Bc5 (unveiling a threat to the queen but sacrificing the exchange) 20. Nxe8 Rxe8 21. Be3 Bxe3 22. fxe3 Qxg3+ 23. Qf2 Rxe3+ (safe from capture because of the queen's pin) 24. Kf1 Qxf2+ 25. Kxf2 Ng4+ 26. Kf1 Nf4, when Black's knights dominate the play.

18.   Bg5   . . .

Kasparov develops his queen-bishop to its optimal square and prepares for queenside castling. At least this plan is better than castling kingside, for after 18. 0-0, Black has Nf6-d5, and the queen-bishop is stuck for a good base of operations.

18.   ...   Ng4

Black could stop White from castling queenside by pushing the queen-bishop pawn to c5. But then the d4-knight would leap to f5, upgrading White's position, with Kasparov still retaining the option of castling kingside.

19.   0-0-0   ...

In general, is it better to castle kingside or queenside? This question can only be answered by applying it to the given circumstances and then making an informed decision.

Kingside castling tends to happen more often because it's easier, there being one piece less to get out of the way. To castle queenside, you must also find something for the queen to do. That's not always such a good idea in the opening.

But when feasible, you should castle queenside if it's natural and makes sense. In deciding which way to go with your king, kingside or queenside, you should regard various factors.

Certainly, timeliness is important. If you must get the king out of the center quickly, or if you need the aid of a rook, you probably want to castle the faster way. But you have to also consider on which side your king will be safer afterward. You wouldn't want to castle into a gathering storm.

Another determining factor is which way contributes most to the attack. You might prefer to castle on the opposite side from your opponent if you sense opportunities to open his position with advances in front of his king. In that event, you wouldn't want your own king exposed and in the way. So if your opponent has castled kingside, you may conclude it's better to castle queenside.

There can be other factors too, such as where the endgame might lead, the way castling affects piece deployments, and how squares are influenced and controlled. There are no automatic rules, so even a computer would have to think about it.

But after Deep Blue's last move, kingside castling is not so safe. With the Black knight hovering at g4, breakthrough sacrifices become possible at h4, followed by a possible queen mate at h2. Kasparov's decision to go queenside is best.

19.   ...   Rhe8

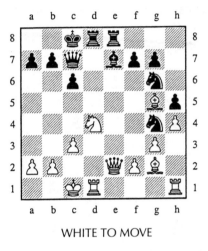

WHITE TO MOVE

Black threatens to win outright by taking the bishop on g5 with check, uncovering an attack to White's queen on e2 along the e-file.

20.   Qc2   ...

The queen shifts out of the danger zone (the e-file), still keeping guard over the f2-pawn and maintaining a protective eye on the entry point at f5.

20.   ...   Kb8

Black removes its king from the c8-h3 diagonal, away from any annoying checks or pins.

21.   Kb1   ...

White prepares to oust the knight from g4. The immediate kick with the bishop-pawn, 21. f3?, fails to 21. . . . Bxg5 + 22. hxg5 Ne3, forking queen and rook. But once White moves his king (Kc1-b1) off the hazardous c1-h6 checking diagonal, advancing the f-pawn up a square to dislodge the knight is on the agenda.

21.   ...   Bxg5

Starting here, Deep Blue begins an operation designed to improve the position of the Black knights. The entire sequence is loaded with tactical barbs, just the sort of thing in which metal mind specializes.

22.   hxg5   N6e5

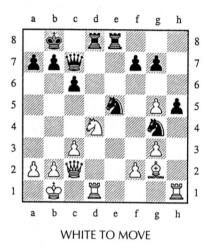

WHITE TO MOVE

Deep Blue's knight has finally branched out from the g6-square, but what about the hanging Black pawn at h5? Can Kasparov just take it for nothing with his rook?

This is going to require some analysis. If 23. Rxh5, then Black follows with 23. . . . c5, forcing a fleeing of the White knight from d4.

If the knight goes to f5, then Black has a pawn fork at g6, winning either knight or rook. If instead the knight goes back to f3, then Black trades rooks on d1, deflecting White's queen from the defense of f2, and Black's g4-knight eats the f-pawn. But what happens if White tries the aggressive 24. Nd4-b5, attacking Black's queen?

Black follows with 24. . . . Qb6, menacing the knight, which can be defended by 25. a4. The key move is then 25. . . . a6, sniping at the b5-knight and driving it back.

White can either retreat the knight to a3, or preface this by first exchanging rooks on d8. However White replies, Black will be able to capture on f2 (Ng4xf2), regaining the pawn, inasmuch as taking the knight with White's queen (Qc2xf2) allows the Black queen to check and fork at g6, winning the errant h5-rook.

Getting back to the question, can Kasparov take the h-pawn, 23. Rh1xh5? Yes, but Black recovers the pawn in a few moves, coming away with decidedly better chances. So the champion makes a very human decision. He wisely turns down the pawn and improves his central position.

23.   Rhe1   . . .

Kasparov, too, is no slouch at calculating variations. With his rook move, Rhe1, he thus sidesteps all of Black's traps. In turn he threatens to trap Deep Blue's g4-knight by advancing the bishop-pawn one square, f2-f3. If the knight then seeks shelter at h2, entering the lion's den, White discovers a winning attack to it along the second rank from the queen by withdrawing his bishop to h1.

23.   . . .   c5

Deep Blue beats White to the punch, countering the threat to its own knight by attacking Kasparov's knight first.

24.   Nf3   . . .

This is the safest withdrawal. By going to either b5 or f5, the knight finds itself in the outlands.

24.   . . .   Rxd1 +

25.   Rxd1   Nc4

Deep Blue continually finds provocative squares on which to place the knights. On c4, the knight cannot be driven back by b2-b3??, for Black has a forking check at a3, winning White's queen.

26.   Qa4   . . .

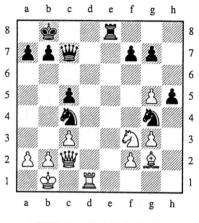

AFTER BLACK'S 25th MOVE

Did Deep Blue miss something? This looks awfully good. Both rook and knight are under attack, but the machine's machinations have taken everything into account.

26.   ...   Rd8

Black's best move. Erroneous would be to retreat the knight to d6, when White could simply take it off with his rook, Rd1xd6, undermining the protection for e8. If Black takes back, Qc7xd6, White's queen cleans up, Qa4xe8 + .

27.   Re1   ...

Curiously, the rooks have exchanged open files. White's was on the d-file, now it's on the e-file. Black's was on the e-file, now it's on the d-file. Who's on first?

Meanwhile, Deep Blue still must decide where to put its attacked c4-knight. If it charges to d2 with check, White exchanges knights, 27. ... Nd2 + 28. Nxd2 Rxd2, invades on the back rank, 28. Re8 + Rd8, and centralizes the queen powerfully, 29. Qe4, threatening to trade rooks on d8 and to mate by capturing on b7 (don't forget the sneaky bishop at g2). And if Black, to avoid this contingency, initiates the trade of rooks itself (himself?/herself?), 29. ... Rxe8 30. Qxe8 + Qc8, White gobbles a pawn, 31. Qxf7.

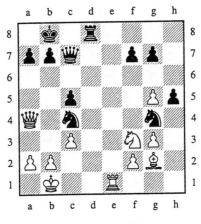

BLACK TO MOVE

Not desirable either is repositioning the knight to e5. If 27. ... Nce5, then 28. Nxe5 Nxe5 29. f4 Nd3 30. Re8 is lovely for White.

Here, the bishop is clearly the superior minor piece. It has long-range access to the Black king, while the knight has lost contact with the vital center squares.

27.   ...   Nb6

28.   Qc2   ...

The queen, having done its dirty work, withdraws to the second rank, standing sentinel over the f2-pawn.

28.   ...   Qd6

The game enters a new phase. Deep Blue's plan is to oppose queens on the b1-h7 diagonal. With White's queen gone or immobilized, the f2-pawn is fodder.

29.   c4   ...

Kasparov makes no attempt to stop Deep Blue from carrying out its plan. Instead he plays to keep Black's queen-knight under wraps by judicious use of the pawns. It's the same strategy he used earlier in the game, when the knight occupied g6.

29.   ...   Qg6

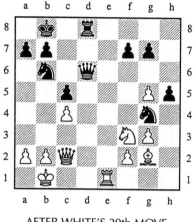

AFTER WHITE'S 29th MOVE

The alternative method of implementing the plan, 29. . . . Qd3, is not so effective. After trading queens, 30. Qxd3 Rxd3, White picks up an essential tempo with his king by 31. Kc2!.

Black's rook will not be able to maintain its forward position by being defended, for if the knight captures the bishop-pawn, 31. . . . Nxf2?, White's rook counterattacks, 32. Re2, undermining the knight's ability to guard the d3-rook. So the rook must retreat, say to d7. But after 31. . . . Rd7 32. b3 Nxf2, White penetrates with 33. Re8+ Kc7 34. Ne5, and Black's counterattack, 34. . . . Rd1, comes too late: 35. Nxf7 Rg1 36. Re7.

For Deep Blue's plan to have any chance of success, it's essential that White's king stand on b1.

30.   Qxg6   . . .

Also possible was 30. b3 Nxf2 31. Qxg6, which is just a transposition of moves. Not acceptable, however, is 30. Re7??, allowing 30. . . . Rd1#—mate! Note that White's queen is pinned and can't capture the rook on d1.

30.   . . .   fxg6

31.   b3   . . .

Still playing to restrict the b6-knight. Deep Blue can have the f2-pawn, for Kasparov sees how he can get it back.

31.   . . .   Nxf2

32.   Re6   . . .

Here 32. Re7 is not so effective. Black opposes rooks, 32. . . . Rd7, and after 33. Re8 + Kc7 34. Ne5, Deep Blue has the nasty check, 34. . . . Rd1 +. White gets out of check, 35. Kc2, but then Black gets real counterplay with 35. . . . Rg1.

32.   . . .   Kc7

Deep Blue cannot save its g-pawn, so it improves the position of its king.

33.   Rxg6   . . .

Kasparov has recovered his pawn and now threatens the g7-pawn, which Deep Blue defends.

33.   . . .   Rd7

34.   Nh4   . . .

Kasparov's game is looking strong. He threatens 33. Nf5, ganging up on the weakling at g7.

34.   . . .   Nc8!

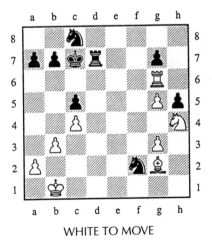

WHITE TO MOVE

A marvelous counter. A human being might find this move following the precept: Improve your worst placed piece. Deep Blue finds it by crunching numbers.

Kasparov must be exceedingly careful here. The tempting 35. Nf5 turns out to be a mistake because of 35. . . . Ne7!, when after 36. Nxe7 Rxe7, White's rook finds itself unexpectedly ensnared. The knight then rounds up the rook, either by 37. . . . Nd3 and 38. . . . Ne5, or by 37. . . . Ng4 and 38. . . . Ne5. Here, the ability of the knight to move to squares of both colors outweighs long-range proclivities of the bishop, which is idle, confined to one color.

35.   Bd5   . . .

Frustrated in his attempt to win the g7-pawn, Kasparov plays to block the d-file. With the Black rook bottled up, Kasparov has time to figure out another plan of attack.

35.   . . .   Nd6

Black's rook may be bottled up, but its knight is breaking free.

36.   Re6   . . .

White terminates his attack on the g-pawn in order to keep the Black knights from e4.

36.   . . .   Nb5!

The final pirouette. The knight threatens entry at c3 or d4. In this game, at least, the knight has proved itself the bishop's equal. Kasparov's next move, allowing the exchange of bishop for knight, acknowledges as much.

37.   cxb5   Rxd5
38.   Rg6   . . .

Back to the old stand. The attack on the g-pawn still offers the best chance to win.

38.   . . .   Rd7

For the time being, Deep Blue holds off on counterattack, taking a moment out to defend the g7-pawn, which it doesn't want to fall with check.

39.   Nf5   Ne4

Both sides move their knights into position, attacking enemy g-pawns.

40.   Nxg7   ...

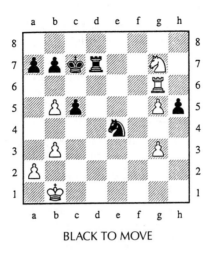

BLACK TO MOVE

The knight ending that arises after 40. Rxg7 Rxg7 41. Nxg7 Nxg3 offers White no winning chances whatsoever. Black's h-pawn is just as dangerous as White's g-pawn. White could even lose after 42. g6? Kd7!.

40.   ...   Rd1 +!

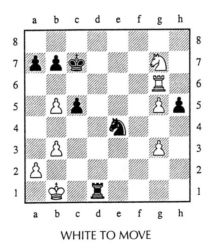

WHITE TO MOVE

The capture 40. . . . Nxg3? would fall into Kasparov's trap. After 41. Ne6 +, Black's king is in a quandary. If it steps back, 41. . . . Kc8, it gets mated by 42. Rg8 + Rd8 43. Rxd8. And if the king comes forward, 41. . . . Kd6, Black loses the exchange to a discovered check, 42. Nf8 + and 43. Nxd7.

The time has come. Deep Blue must start a counteroffensive.

41.   Kc2   Rd2 +

42.   Kc1   . . .

And not 42. Kb1, which would allow Deep Blue to set up a drawing mechanism by 42. . . . Nc3 + 43. Kc1 (not king to the corner, 43. Ka1??, because the rook captures with mate, 43. . . . Rxa2#) 43. . . . Re2. Once the rook and knight are in their proper positions, there is no way to stop perpetual check (actually a draw by threefold repetition). The knight simply goes from c3 to a2 to c3 to a2, and Black claims a draw.

42.   . . .   Rxa2

Clearly, Black's rook must be disengaged from the attack of White's king. Otherwise, its knight is frozen on e4, defending the rook. It could try 42. . . . Re2, attempting to set up the drawing configuration just shown, but 43. Ne6 + Kd7 44. Nf4 upsets the applecart. Now Black has nothing better than 44. . . . Rxa2 anyway, but the loss of time has allowed White to improve his chances.

Kasparov's task is to move his rook and knight away, to unobstruct the g-pawn so that it can advance. Since the rook can't move without abandoning g5 to Black's knight, it's the knight that must move to safety first.

43.   Nxh5   . . .

The safest move. Kasparov eliminates the Black h-pawn, while guarding his own g-pawn.

43.   . . .   Nd2

Kasparov has a passed pawn, the g-pawn, and Deep Blue wants (can it want?) a passed pawn too. The idea is 44. . . . Nxb3 +, and the c5-pawn becomes a passer.

44.   Nf4   . . .

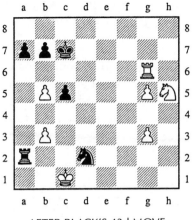

AFTER BLACK'S 43d MOVE

Here, it would appear, is the right moment for Kasparov to move his rook and unblock the g-pawn's advance. Instead, he chooses another safe move, placing the knight on a protected square and returning it to play. The g6-rook will move soon enough.

44. . . .   Nxb3 +

Deep Blue follows through, removing the White b3-pawn, rendering the Black c-pawn passed and hot to trot.

45. Kb1   . . .

Best. Running to the kingside with 45. Kd1? lets Deep Blue's pawn come on too fast.

45. . . .   Rd2

The rook moves to safety, observing the central d5-square, where White might like to position his knight. Another point, Kasparov's king is stalemated (though it is not stalemate, for White has moves with things other than his king). But, since White's king has no move, a check will do it in.

46. Re6   . . .

The White rook finally makes its move, and at last the g-pawn is ready to run. So, too, is the Black c-pawn.

46. . . .   c4

Threatening 47. . . . c3 and 48. . . . Rb2#. White must recall his rook to cover the c3-square.

47.   Re3   . . .

The rook has to do the job of controlling c3. Returning the knight, 47. Ne2, abandons control of d5. And Black's rook promptly steps up, 47. . . . Rd5, where it will pick off the White b5-pawn and still have time to come back to g5 to keep watch over the g-pawn.

47.   . . .   Kb6

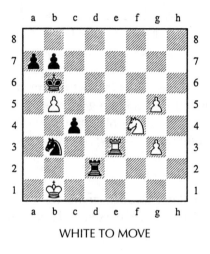

WHITE TO MOVE

One thing that distinguishes the endgame from the other two phases (the opening and middlegame) is use of the king. For safety, it's usually tucked away in a corner by castling in the opening. But once the queen and a few other pieces disappear from the board, there's less danger of suddenly being checkmated.

It therefore makes sense to empower the king as soon as the endgame begins, bringing it back to civilization, so to speak. After all, it has both attacking and defensive muscle, circumambiently guarding all the squares in its immediate area. The strong player knows that employing this valuable weapon may be the very step needed to win or save the game.

Starting here, the game moves into its final stage. The Black king will march down the board, looking to entrap its White counterpart. Simultaneously, the White g-pawn will rush up the board, hoping to promote.

48.	g6	Kxb5
49.	g7	Kb4!

And the players agreed to a draw. The match remains tied after five games, 2.5–2.5, with three draws and one win each.

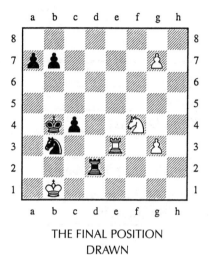

THE FINAL POSITION
DRAWN

A sudden and dramatic conclusion, which took everyone by surprise. After White queens his pawn, 50. g8/Q, Black forces perpetual check by 50. . . . Rd1 + 51. Kc2 Rd2 + 52. Kb1 Rd1 +, etc.

Many players might have stopped their analysis once they realized the g-pawn promotes, thereby overlooking this great resource. Being suddenly behind by a queen is enough to dissuade anyone from looking further. But not a supercomputer, which considers everything on its horizon. In this case, quantity became quality. The machine won over many converts, artfully fashioning a solution that speaks to the poetry of the game.

The match is tied 2.5–2.5.

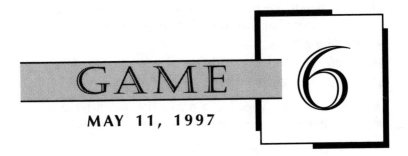

GAME 6

MAY 11, 1997

WHITE: **Deep Blue**

BLACK: **Garry Kasparov**

OPENING: **Caro-Kann Defense**

ECO CODE: **B17**

RESULT: **Deep Blue wins in 19 moves**

SCORE: **Deep Blue 3.5—Kasparov 2.5**
      Deep Blue wins match

THE MOVES

NO.	WHITE	BLACK	NO.	WHITE	BLACK
1.	e4	c6	11.	Bf4	b5
2.	d4	d5	12.	a4	Bb7
3.	Nc3	dxe4	13.	Re1	Nd5
4.	Nxe4	Nd7	14.	Bg3	Kc8
5.	Ng5	Ngf6	15.	axb5	cxb5
6.	Bd3	e6	16.	Qd3	Bc6
7.	N1f3	h6	17.	Bf5	exf5
8.	Nxe6	Qe7	18.	Rxe7	Bxe7
9.	0-0	fxe6	19.	c4	Black resigns
10.	Bg6 +	Kd8		(1–0)	

DEEP SIXED BY DEEP BLUE

What can we say about this game? It will undoubtedly go down as one of the most famous games in the annals of chess. Not only because it's the worst beating world-champion Kasparov has ever suffered, but also for its import in the history of civilization.

The opening began as a Caro-Kann Defense, which Kasparov had experimented with in his earlier years. It quickly reached a point where the champion allowed Deep Blue to make a familiar sacrifice of a knight for attack. Since the gambit is widely known, did Kasparov allow it because he had discovered a refutation?

If he had, it's still a well-kept secret. Deep Blue wasted no time taking command. Forcing Black's king to move, the machine reduced the Black forces to an inarticulate huddle, with pieces stumbling over each other.

With the noose tightening around his neck, and Deep Blue about to pounce on some good material, Kasparov tried a last-ditch queen sacrifice, hoping to break the attack and turn the game around. But Deep Blue consumed the queen without relinquishing the fury of its attack, and after a cutting pawn move, the champ's position was in ruins.

In unceremonious fashion, after having played a mere eighteen moves over a period of only an hour, Garry Kasparov, the strongest human chess player of all time, got up from the playing table, resigned, and walked off in a huff. He had lost the game, the match, a pile of money, and a great deal of prestige. Forever after, he will be remembered as the first chess champion to be trounced by a supercomputer.

	White Deep Blue		Black Garry Kasparov
1.	**e4**	**c6**	
2.	**d4**	**d5**	

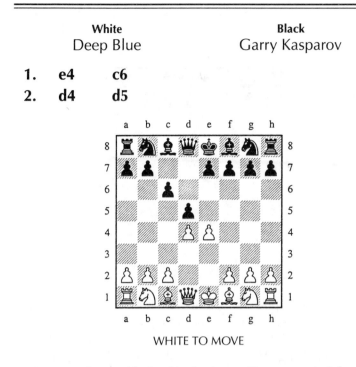

WHITE TO MOVE

In game four, with the Black pieces, Kasparov tried the little creeping move, d7-d6. Here, in the final and decisive sixth game of the match, he returns to the opening of his youth, the solid Caro-Kann Defense.

And here the computer must decide what to do about its attacked e4-pawn. Deep Blue can advance it, 3. e5, exchange it, 3. exd5, or protect it.

3.   Nc3   . . .

The traditional method of guarding the e4-pawn. White develops its queen-knight to its optimal square. Even today, this old respected move is considered to be White's most promising course.

3.   . . .   dxe4

Kasparov exchanges pawns, releasing the tension in the center. There is really nothing better. For the attempt to increase the pressure on the e4-square by 3. . . . Nf6 is strongly answered by 4. e5, attacking the knight.

4.   Nxe4   . . .

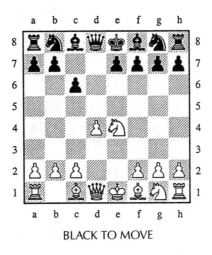

BLACK TO MOVE

The standard position of the Caro-Kann Defense has been attained. With both a pawn and a knight in the center, White has the makings of a positional advantage. Clearly, Black must begin to challenge White for control of central points, and this is done in the Caro by going after the e4-knight.

The original method of Horatio Caro (1862–1920) and Marcus Kann (1820–86) was to develop the king-knight, 4. . . . Nf6, forcing the e4-knight to come to a decision: either back off or exchange.

Normally, White will opt for the exchange, 5. Nxf6 + , when Black will have to recapture with either the e-pawn or the g-pawn, concomitantly accepting doubled pawns. While there is nothing terribly wrong with this line, it has fallen out of fashion. Most modern masters prefer not to incur doubled f-pawns if they don't have to.

A second method is to play 4. . . . Bf5, developing the queen-bishop with attack on the e4-knight. The world champion of the 1920s, José Raúl Capablanca (1888–1942), set a certain vogue for the bishop move when he used it in back-to-back games in the New York 1927 tournament.

Capa's move, 4. . . . Bf5, has been dubbed the Main Line,

and to this day, it's still considered Black's most solid line in the Caro. The one drawback is that Black has very few chances to win. He can usually make a draw, but winning requires that White overplay his hand.

Finally, there is the method used by Kasparov in the present game. It's a refined way of getting the knight to f6, without shouldering the doubling of f-pawns.

4.   ...   Nd7

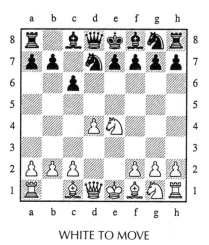

WHITE TO MOVE

This move also has a long pedigree: Aaron Nimzovich (1886–1935) in the 1920s, Salo Flohr (1908–83) in the 1930s, world champions Tigran Petrosian (1929–84) and Vassily Smyslov (1921–) in the 1950s and 1960s, and in the 1980s, Anatoly Karpov (1951–), Kasparov's predecessor on the chess throne.

The idea behind moving the knight to d7 is clear. Black intends to develop the other knight to f6, and in the event White's knight takes Black's, the d7-knight recaptures, preserving Black's pawn structure. If there is a drawback to Black's knight move, it's the hemming in of the c8-bishop.

5.   Ng5   ...

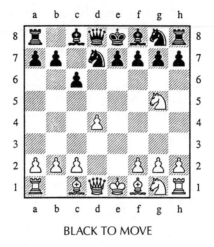

BLACK TO MOVE

A strange-looking move, of the kind you would expect a computer to play. Sorry to disappoint you, but humans were there first.

The knight move first attracted attention when it was played in a quarter finals candidates match for the women's world championship, at Bad Kissengen in 1983. White won.

At the time, it was merely a footnote on the pages of opening theory. But then, three years later, the men began to take notice, and from a footnote, it grew into a main line.

It should be said that the move Ne4-g5 was not a completely unknown idea. It had been seen in a slightly different setting, after 5. Bc4 Ngf6, and then 6. Ng5.

Here the idea of the knight move is to attack the f7-square. And after 6. . . . e6 7. Qe2, Black has to be alert and play 7. . . . Nb6! If he tries to chase the obstreperous knight with 7. . . . h6?, he gets poleaxed by 8. Nxf7! Kxf7 9. Qxe6+ Kg6 10. Bd3+ Kh5 11. Qh3#. This is not nice, but it illustrates the problems Black has in pushing the knight out of his half of the board. These same difficulties crop up in the present game.

Should Black now play 5. . . . h6, the knight does not have to retreat. Instead, White can boldly play 6. Ne6!, daring Black to

Although the origins of chess are lost in antiquity, the history of the world chess championship can be easily traced. Garry Kasparov, the current world champion, is the thirteenth in line since 1886, when the first official championship match between J. H. Zukertort and Wilhelm Steinitz was held in three North American cities, New York, St. Louis, and New Orleans.

The winner of that event, the Prague-born Steinitz (1836–1900), held the title for eight years until he was defeated by Emanuel Lasker (1868–1941) of Germany in 1894. Lasker retained the top spot longer than anyone else, keeping it for twenty-seven years. In 1921 the older Lasker was beaten soundly by the Cuban phenomenon, José Raúl Capablanca (1888–1942), who in turn lost it to Alexander Alekhine (1892–1946) of Russia in 1927. Alekhine dropped it in 1935 to Max Euwe (1901–81) of Holland, who lost it back to Alekhine in 1937. Alekhine kept the title until his death in 1946, the only man to die as champion.

In 1948 a special world-championship tournament was contested between six of the planet's best players, and it was won convincingly by Mikhail Botvinnik (1911–94) of the Soviet Union. Botvinnik lost and regained the title several times, before forever relinquishing it in 1963.

Vassily Smyslov (1921–) held it from 1957–58, Mikhail Tal (1936–91) held it from 1960–61, Tigran Petrosian (1929–84) held it from 1963–69, and Boris Spassky (1937–) held it from 1969–72, until he was annihilated by Bobby Fischer (1943–) at Reykjavik in 1972, the event that still remains the greatest chess spectacle of all time.

The American-born mercurial Fischer never played a single game as champion, losing the title in 1975 by forfeit to Anatoly Karpov (1951–) of the Soviet Union. Karpov dominated the chess arena until 1985, when he was defeated by his nemesis, Garry Kasparov (1963–), who has held the world's top spot ever since, with even greater command than Karpov.

Garry Kasparov, the thirteenth and last human world champion, has never lost a match since assuming the title in 1985. Until now.

capture: 6. . . . fxe6?? 7. Qh5+ g6 8. Qxg6#, a version of the Fool's Mate.

The Fool's Mate, not named after anyone in particular, is one of the best-known finales in all chess. In its simplest form it refers to the shortest game possible, two moves, and it's White who loses. For example, 1. f3? e5 2. g4?? Qh4#.

There are other ways it can come about as well, so in a more general sense it denotes any checkmate occurring along the king-side diagonal leading to the king on its original square. The Black king would be mated along the e8-h5 diagonal, and the White king would be mated along the e1-h4 diagonal.

The crazy thing about the two-move variant of the Fool's Mate, is that most people think, to win this quickly, one has to be a good player. But as you can see, being good has nothing to do with it. The loser loses because he plays the two worst moves on the board, without any provocation from the other player, nor any relation to his opponent's moves whatsoever.

Another sad tale, where Black held up on the capture for a few moves, was Nunn vs. Kir. Georgiev, Linares 1988. It went: 5. . . . h6 6. Ne6 Qa5+ 7. Bd2 Qb6 8. Bd3 fxe6?? 9. Qh5+ Kd8 10. Ba5!, and Black lost his queen because of the pin.

You should also be aware that in response to 4. . . . Nd7, White has some perfectly good, normal-looking moves, namely 5. Nf3, 5. Bd3, and 5. Bc4. Plus there is the nasty trap that has caught many players napping: 5. Qe2!? Ngf6?? 6. Nd6#, a smothered mate. Try not to fall for that one.

5.   ...   Ngf6

The pesky White knight cannot so easily be chased away. So Kasparov develops his knight, and in so doing, takes control of the h5-square, which White's queen is now unable to use.

6.   Bd3   ...

Again it appears that Black is ready to kick the knight by 6. . . . h6. Not so! The stem game, Semenova vs. Muresan, saw

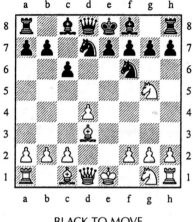

BLACK TO MOVE

6. . . . h6? 7. Ne6!, and the knight is immune, for 7. . . . fxe6?? Is met by 8. Bg6#.

6.   ...   e6

Kasparov continues to play natural moves. The king gets some breathing room, and the f8-bishop has a clear path to come out. The big drawback: the c8-bishop does not get to emerge off the home rank, locked in by the e6-pawn.

7.   N1f3   ...

White also continues with natural developing moves, but at last Black can seriously consider h7-h6.

7.   ...   h6?!

Well, maybe not. The most reliable move is thought to be 7. . . . Bd6. Then, after 8. Qe2, Black can safely play 8. . . . h6, which is the move he's been looking to play all along. But what happens if Black moves the rook-pawn on move seven, as Kasparov does here?

8.   Nxe6!   ...

The knight still goes forward into Black's camp, sacrificing itself to expose the enemy king. Even at a couple hundred mil-

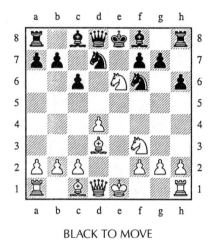

BLACK TO MOVE

lion positions a second, Deep Blue would have an impossible task crunching through all the moves, calculating all the contingent variations, and then trying to evaluate them. Fortunately, it doesn't have to.

All that is required is for Deep Blue to consult its opening book, electronically of course. There, on the appropriate page where this exact position occurs, it will find the move embedded by theory: 8. Nxe6, with or without the exclamation mark.

For Kasparov, too, the knight sacrifice is not an unknown quantity. It is stored away in his memory cells with the evaluation: "Very dangerous move for Black." So why allow it?

The thinking in the Kasparov camp was likely that after the sac, Deep Blue constantly would be analyzing positions in which it would find itself behind in material. In view of the high value the computer places on material point count, Deep Blue might not be able to evaluate correctly the true attacking potential of White's position. It's a very risky gamble, especially the way Deep Blue has played overall in this match.

8.   ...   Qe7

Kasparov adopts the main move, pinning the e6-knight and vacating the square d8 for his king, in anticipation of the coming bishop check at g6. The alternative, which nobody really trusts, is the immediate capture of the knight by 8. . . . fxe6.

Then, in response to 9. Bg6 +, Black's king must take up a clumsy stance on e7. Still, this line has its points, for after 9. . . . Ke7 10. 0-0, Black can play 10. . . . Qc7, preventing White's queen-bishop from playing to its appropriate square, f4. Later, the Black king can drop back to d8, and the f8-bishop can be developed at d6.

This was the course of Wolff vs. Zuniga, New York 1994, a game that Black managed to win after many adventures.

9.   0-0   . . .

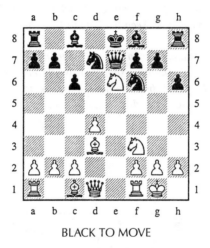

BLACK TO MOVE

The tricky but timely castling move, where you get to move two pieces on the same turn, and it's not considered cheating. In case you haven't heard, castling is advisable, and here it's more than that. It's the only good move.

Deep Blue, by castling, removes its king from the dangerous open e-file, unpinning its e6-knight in the process. Moreover, its king-rook is now ready to take part in the proceedings.

9.   . . .   fxe6

The White knight was threatening to play to c7, forking Black's king and rook. It had to be taken before it could do more damage. And it had to be taken with the pawn. For 9. . . . Qxe6 is out of the question, due to the resulting pin along the e-file, 10. Re1, when Black can kiss his queenly Penelope good-bye for the last time.

10.   Bg6+   ...

An essential follow-up to the knight sacrifice. The Black king must move toward the center, forfeiting the castling privilege, and the Black g-pawn is held in place, jamming up Black's forces.

> One of the aims of the opening is to delay or actually prevent the other side from castling. Keep the king in the center and it becomes the fox in a hunt.
>
> There are various ways to do this, including tying the king down to defensive chores, guarding squares it would have to pass over in the act of castling, and therefore can't, and making it move. Once the king moves, it forfeits the right to castle, even if it goes back to its original square.

10.   ...   Kd8

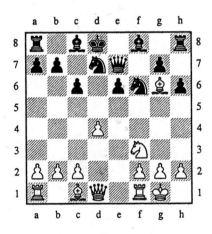

WHITE TO MOVE

Kasparov's king scurries to its only safe square. It's another question altogether if the Black king will find permanent security on d8. The answer, based on prior experience, is probably not.

11. Bf4   . . .

The main-line move, the one most often played in past published games. The bishop takes up its appropriate post on f4, cutting across the center and aiming in the direction of Black's king.

More recently, the game Leko vs. Bakhtazde, Las Palmas 1995, saw another eleventh move for White, c2-c4, and this could prove to be even stronger. The continuation of the game shows that Black had enormous problems to solve: 11. c4 Qd6 12. Qe2 Qc7 13. Rd1 Bd6 14. Ne5 Rf8 15. Bf4 Bxe5 16. dxe5 Ng8 17. Bg3 Qb6 18. Qg4 c5 19. Rd6 Qxb2 20. Rad1 Kc7 21. Qxe6 Ndf6 22. Rd7 + !, and Black resigned.

Back to the present game.

11. . . .   b5

The first brand-new move of the day. Home preparation or over-the-board inspiration? Only Garry Kasparov knows for sure.

The idea is clear, to stop White from getting c2-c4. In this way Black secures the d5-square, where he later intends to play the f6-knight.

Additionally, Kasparov can begin the process of untangling his queenside pieces. The bishop at c8, which up to now had no squares to move to, can start to get around town.

It's unlikely that Kasparov's move changes the essentials of the position in any significant way. The Black army is just too undeveloped, crammed into a tiny space behind its own lines. The White forces meanwhile are free to roam over the entire board, and can potshot any Black unit that sticks its head out.

12. a4   . . .

Deep Blue is now completely on its own. There is no more book to follow, and the advice of the a-pawn was generated by its own internal circuitry.

The move that Deep Blue has self-produced is excellent.

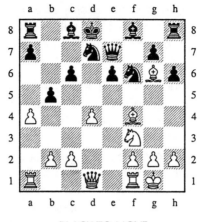

BLACK TO MOVE

Kasparov's last play has provided a target, and the computer loses no time bringing the b5-pawn into its sights.

The immediate import is not so much to win the b-pawn, which is presently guarded. Rather, the purpose is to open the a-file for White's rook.

This can occur in two ways. Black can take White's a-pawn, b5xa4, or White can take Black's b-pawn, a4xb5. In either case, the a-file is opened to the a1-rook, which becomes active without having to be moved from its starting berth.

Activating the rooks is something only White can accomplish in the current position. Kasparov's rooks, at least for the near future, are stuck in the corners.

12.   . . .   Bb7

Kasparov continues as planned, lifting his bishop off its home square. There's the possibility that, if an exchange takes place on b5, the diagonal of Black's b7-bishop could be cleared of debris.

13.   Re1   . . .

Deep Blue continues to pile on the pressure by increasing the scope of its rooks. This is something the champ cannot counter, with his rooks at opposite poles. First White's queen-rook is given a shot along the a-file, then the king-rook usurps the e-file. Moreover, there's the ghastly Black pawn on e6, with its spectral presence, held solely by Black's burdened queen.

13.   ...   Nd5

Kasparov assuages the position of his king-knight, impressing it on the board's center. From d5, the knight strikes out at the unguarded f4-bishop.

14.   Bg3   ...

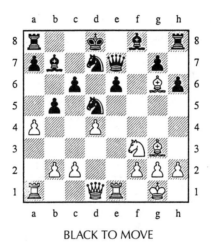

BLACK TO MOVE

The bishop calmly withdraws, maintaining its menacing demeanor along the b8-h2 diagonal.

14.   ...   Kc8

It's a bad sign when the world champion, as early as move fourteen, is reduced to sliding his king one square. It means that Kasparov's position is so disorganized that useful moves can't be found, at least not without the aid of a computer.

The d7-knight is glued to its post, having to stand guard over the e5-square, where White would relish placing its knight.

Ideally, Black would like to flee e7 with his queen, permitting the f8-bishop to come out. But where can the queen go? If it moves to b4, the king-pawn drops to White's rook, Re1xe6, which is then positioned to threaten mate at e8. And if the queen tries f6, it gets pinned by the bishop at h4. So what's left? A king move.

15.   axb5   . . .

Time to blast open the a-file.

15.   . . .   cxb5

A forced recapture.

16.   Qd3   . . .

White develops the queen with tempo, assailing the pawn on b5. Black doesn't have the luxury of being able to move his queen.

16.   . . .   Bc6

Kasparov protects the b5-pawn with his bishop, at the same time preparing a refuge for his king at b7.

17.   Bf5!   . . .

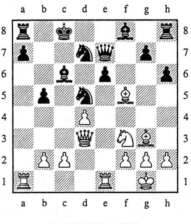

BLACK TO MOVE

Simple and strong. The e6-pawn is brought under fire, and it's hard to find a viable defense.

17.   . . .   exf5

Unable to defend the e6-pawn, Kasparov returns the material, hoping to break the force of White's onslaught. So he surrenders his queen for practical material equivalence.

18.   Rxe7   Bxe7

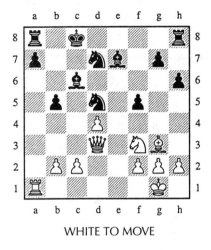

WHITE TO MOVE

Nominally, material is close to even. Black has two minor pieces for the queen and a couple of pawns. There's even a threat to trap the g3-bishop by f5-f4.

But the reality is something quite different, for material is not the main issue. What's at stake is the coordination of the Black forces, the safety of the Black king, and, perhaps, the dignity and supremacy of humankind.

White's entire army is in play. The Black forces are in disarray. The Black king looks pale. The future seems bleak. It's time to buy IBM stock.

19.   c4!   . . .
Black resigns (1–0)

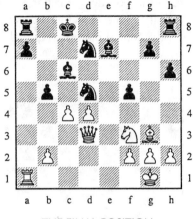

THE FINAL POSITION

Deep Blue wins the match, 3.5–2.5.

For fans of Kasparov, everything was gone with the win.

In referring to Deep Blue throughout, we have also alluded to members of its team. On a human level, many people can take credit for the computer's success, but several stand out as being cardinal.

Chung-Jen Tan is the project manager, and Feng-Hsiung Hsu is presently Deep Blue's principal designer. Also paramount are programming scientists Murray Campbell, Joseph Hoane Jr., and Jerry Brody. Finally, on the chess side, grandmaster Joel Benjamin did a fantastic job overseeing Deep Blue's preparation and game plan.

AFTERWORD

So what's it all about? What really happened? What does it mean?

Hey, it's only a chess match that was lost. Nothing more, nothing less. True, but the match was lost not by just anyone, but by the world champion, and not to just anyone, but to a machine.

Deep Blue won the match, but does this mean that IBM's supercomputer is a stronger chess player than Garry Kasparov? Most experts don't think so. Ask around and almost unanimously they say Kasparov is still superior, though they admit the gap is narrowing.

But isn't the winner better by definition? None of us really believe this, especially when it's our favorite player or team that loses. Were the Pittsburgh Pirates of 1960 actually better than the team they defeated in the World Series, the awesome New York Yankees of 1960? Are you kidding?

Of course, chess isn't a team sport, yet wasn't it a team of specialists that put Deep Blue in position to win? On one level, the battle is human versus machine. But on another, isn't it also one of individual thinking against collective intelligence?

So why *did* Kasparov lose? Surely, he was enervated. Most authorities believe that Garry simply wore himself out trying to fool the computer with all those bizarre openings. He got advantageous positions but exhausted himself in the process, working out the intricacies of unfamiliar lines. After five of these intense struggles, over a mere eight days, Kasparov had nothing left for that fateful sixth game, and it showed.

Another source of trouble for Kasparov was his own emotions. It's hard watching the man play without becoming fascinated by his body language and facial expressions. We can laugh at them, but these same gestures are notorious for scaring his opponents to death. They had no effect on the machine, and Garry wasn't able to learn from its reactions. Only Deep Blue's operators were intimidated.

Let's also give credit to those operators and to Deep Blue itself. This machine was twice as powerful as the previous version, more responsive to adjustments between games, and better equipped to evaluate nuances and abstruse chess situations.

But the truth is, Kasparov lost simply because he didn't play his best. In fact, he didn't even play like Kasparov, and that was the problem. With his eccentric choice of openings, and his overcaution, he fought without his greatest weapons, his courage and brilliance. These qualities were not there, and with their absence went the champion's chances.

Kasparov forgot the most basic principle to success: be true to yourself. Polonius was right, and he may never have won a chess match.

THE GAMES OF MATCH ONE:

KASPAROV

◆

DEEP BLUE I

The following are the six games of the first match played between Garry Kasparov and Deep Blue, at Philadelphia, in February of 1996. That match was won going away by Kasparov, 4–2.

GAME 1

PHILADELPHIA ◆ 1996

□ DEEP BLUE ■ KASPAROV

1.e4 c5 2.c3 d5 3.exd5 Qxd5 4.d4 Nf6 5.Nf3
Bg4 6.Be2 e6 7.h3 Bh5 8.0-0 Nc6 9.Be3 cxd4
10.cxd4 Bb4 11.a3 Ba5 12.Nc3 Qd6 13.Nb5 Qe7
14.Ne5 Bxe2 15.Qxe2 0-0 16.Rac1 Rac8 17.Bg5
Bb6 18.Bxf6 gxf6 19.Nc4 Rfd8 20.Nxb6 axb6
21.Rfd1 f5 22.Qe3 Qf6 23.d5 Rxd5 24.Rxd5 exd5
25.b3 Kh8 26.Qxb6 Rg8 27.Qc5 d4 28.Nd6 f4
29.Nxb7 Ne5 30.Qd5 f3 31.g3 Nd3 32.Rc7 Re8
33.Nd6 Re1+ 34.Kh2 Nxf2 35.Nxf7+ Kg7
36.Ng5+ Kh6 37.Rxh7+

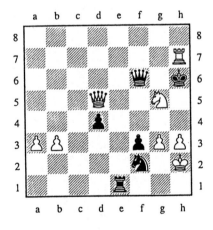

BLACK RESIGNS
1-0

GAME 2

PHILADELPHIA • 1996

□ KASPAROV ■ DEEP BLUE

1.Nf3 d5   2.d4   e6   3.g3   c5   4.Bg2   Nc6   5.0-0   Nf6
6.c4   dxc4   7.Ne5   Bd7   8.Na3   cxd4   9.Naxc4   Bc5
10.Qb3   0-0   11.Qxb7   Nxe5   12.Nxe5   Rb8   13.Qf3
Bd6   14.Nc6   Bxc6   15.Qxc6   e5   16.Rb1   Rb6   17.Qa4
Qb8   18.Bg5   Be7   19.b4   Bxb4   20.Bxf6   gxf6   21.Qd7
Qc8   22.Qxa7   Rb8   23.Qa4   Bc3   24.Rxb8   Qxb8
25.Be4   Qc7   26.Qa6   Kg7   27.Qd3   Rb8   28.Bxh7   Rb2
29.Be4   Rxa2   30.h4   Qc8   31.Qf3   Ra1   32.Rxa1   Bxa1
33.Qh5   Qh8   34.Qg4+   Kf8   35.Qc8+   Kg7   36.Qg4+
Kf8   37.Bd5   Ke7   38.Bc6   Kf8   39.Bd5   Ke7   40.Qf3
Bc3   41.Bc4   Qc8   42.Qd5   Qe6   43.Qb5   Qd7
44.Qc5+   Qd6   45.Qa7+   Qd7   46.Qa8   Qc7
47.Qa3+   Qd6   48.Qa2   f5   49.Bxf7   e4   50.Bh5   Qf6
51.Qa3+   Kd7   52.Qa7+   Kd8   53.Qb8+   Kd7
54.Be8+   Ke7   55.Bb5   Bd2   56.Qc7+   Kf8   57.Bc4
Bc3   58.Kg2   Be1   59.Kf1   Bc3   60.f4   exf3   61.exf3
Bd2   62.f4   Ke8   63.Qc8+   Ke7   64.Qc5+   Kd8
65.Bd3   Be3   66.Qxf5   Qc6   67.Qf8+   Kc7   68.Qe7+
Kc8   69.Bf5+   Kb8   70.Qd8+   Kb7   71.Qd7+   Qxd7
72.Bxd7   Kc7   73.Bb5

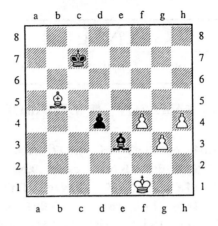

BLACK RESIGNS
1–0

GAME 3

PHILADELPHIA ◆ 1996

□ DEEP BLUE ■ KASPAROV

1.e4 c5 2.c3 d5 3.exd5 Qxd5 4.d4 Nf6 5.Nf3
Bg4 6.Be2 e6 7.0-0 Nc6 8.Be3 cxd4 9.cxd4 Bb4
10.a3 Ba5 11.Nc3 Qd6 12.Ne5 Bxe2 13.Qxe2
Bxc3 14.bxc3 Nxe5 15.Bf4 Nf3+ 16.Qxf3 Qd5
17.Qd3 Rc8 18.Rfc1 Qc4 19.Qxc4 Rxc4 20.Rab1
b6 21.Bb8 Ra4 22.Rb4 Ra5 23.Rc4 0-0 24.Bd6
Ra8 25.Rc6 b5 26.Kf1 Ra4 27.Rb1 a6 28.Ke2 h5
29.Kd3 Rd8 30.Be7 Rd7 31.Bxf6 gxf6 32.Rb3 Kg7
33.Ke3 e5 34.g3 exd4+ 35.cxd4 Re7+ 36.Kf3 Rd7
37.Rd3 Raxd4 38.Rxd4 Rxd4 39.Rxa6 b4

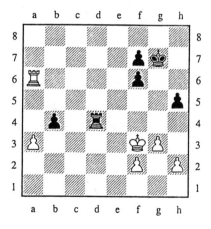

DRAWN BY AGREEMENT
½-½

GAME 4

PHILADELPHIA • 1996

□ KASPAROV ■ DEEP BLUE

1.Nf3 d5 2.d4 c6 3.c4 e6 4.Nbd2 Nf6 5.e3
Nbd7 6.Bd3 Bd6 7.e4 dxe4 8.Nxe4 Nxe4 9.Bxe4
0-0 10.0-0 h6 11.Bc2 e5 12.Re1 exd4 13.Qxd4
Bc5 14.Qc3 a5 15.a3 Nf6 16.Be3 Bxe3 17.Rxe3
Bg4 18.Ne5 Re8 19.Rae1 Be6 20.f4 Qc8 21.h3 b5
22.f5 Bxc4 23.Nxc4 bxc4 24.Rxe8+ Nxe8 25.Re4
Nf6 26.Rxc4 Nd5 27.Qe5 Qd7 28.Rg4 f6 29.Qd4
Kh7 30.Re4 Rd8 31.Kh1 Qc7 32.Qf2 Qb8 33.Ba4
c5 34.Bc6 c4 35.Rxc4 Nb4 36.Bf3 Nd3 37.Qh4
Qxb2 38.Qg3 Qxa3 39.Rc7 Qf8 40.Ra7 Ne5
41.Rxa5 Qf7 42.Rxe5 fxe5 43.Qxe5 Re8 44.Qf4
Qf6 45.Bh5 Rf8 46.Bg6+ Kh8 47.Qc7 Qd4 48.Kh2
Ra8 49.Bh5 Qf6 50.Bg6 Rg8

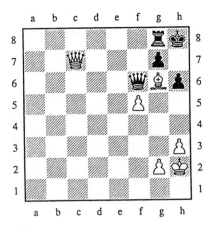

DRAWN BY AGREEMENT
½-½

GAME 5

PHILADELPHIA ◆ 1996

□ **DEEP BLUE**   ■ **KASPAROV**

1.e4   e5   2.Nf3   Nf6   3.Nc3   Nc6   4.d4   exd4   5.Nxd4
Bb4   6.Nxc6   bxc6   7.Bd3   d5   8.exd5   cxd5   9.0–0
0–0   10.Bg5   c6   11.Qf3   Be7   12.Rae1   Re8   13.Ne2
h6   14.Bf4   Bd6   15.Nd4   Bg4   16.Qg3   Bxf4   17.Qxf4
Qb6   18.c4   Bd7   19.cxd5   cxd5   20.Rxe8+   Rxe8
21.Qd2   Ne4   22.Bxe4   dxe4   23.b3   Rd8   24.Qc3   f5
25.Rd1   Be6   26.Qe3   Bf7   27.Qc3   f4   28.Rd2   Qf6
29.g3   Rd5   30.a3   Kh7   31.Kg2   Qe5   32.f3   e3
33.Rd3   e2   34.gxf4   e1Q   35.fxe5   Qxc3   36.Rxc3
Rxd4   37.b4   Bc4   38.Kf2   g5   39.Re3   Be6   40.Rc3
Bc4   41.Re3   Rd2+   42.Ke1   Rd3   43.Kf2   Kg6   44.Rxd3
Bxd3   45.Ke3   Bc2   46.Kd4   Kf5   47.Kd5   h5

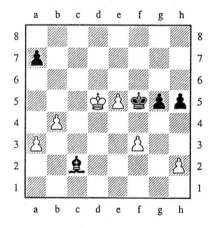

WHITE RESIGNS
0–1

GAME 6

PHILADELPHIA • 1996

□ KASPAROV ■ DEEP BLUE

1.Nf3 d5 2.d4 c6 3.c4 e6 4.Nbd2 Nf6 5.e3 c5
6.b3 Nc6 7.Bb2 cxd4 8.exd4 Be7 9.Rc1 0–0
10.Bd3 Bd7 11.0–0 Nh5 12.Re1 Nf4 13.Bb1 Bd6
14.g3 Ng6 15.Ne5 Rc8 16.Nxd7 Qxd7 17.Nf3 Bb4
18.Re3 Rfd8 19.h4 Nge7 20.a3 Ba5 21.b4 Bc7
22.c5 Re8 23.Qd3 g6 24.Re2 Nf5 25.Bc3 h5
26.b5 Nce7 27.Bd2 Kg7 28.a4 Ra8 29.a5 a6
30.b6 Bb8 31.Bc2 Nc6 32.Ba4 Re7 33.Bc3 Ne5
34.dxe5 Qxa4 35.Nd4 Nxd4 36.Qxd4 Qd7 37.Bd2
Re8 38.Bg5 Rc8 39.Bf6+ Kh7 40.c6 bxc6 41.Qc5
Kh6 42.Rb2 Qb7 43.Rb4

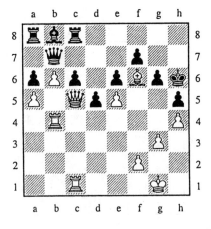

BLACK RESIGNS

1–0

SOURCES

The following is a listing of the various sources for the information presented in this book.

The New York Times, articles by Robert Byrne and Bruce Weber

America Online, commentary by Yasser Seirawan

On-site commentary by Yasser Seirawan, Maurice Ashley, and Mike Valvo

Match Bulletins by Malcolm Pein, Neil McDonald, and Chris Duncan

Personal conversations with various analysts, including Walter Shipman, John Fedorowitz, Nick DeFirmian, Michael Wilder, Tag Taghian, and John Fernandez

ABOUT THE AUTHOR

BRUCE PANDOLFINI is the author of twenty instructional chess books, including *The Chess Doctor; Chess Thinking; Chess Target Practice; More Chess Openings: Traps and Zaps 2; Beginning Chess; Pandolfini's Chess Complete; Chessercizes; More Chessercizes; Checkmate!; Principles of the New Chess; Pandolfini's Endgame Course; Russian Chess; The ABC's of Chess; Let's Play Chess; Kasparov's Winning Chess Tactics; One-Move Chess by the Champions; Chess Openings: Traps and Zaps; Square One; Power Mates: Essential Checkmating Strategies and Techniques;* and *Weapons of Chess.* He is also the editor of the distinguished anthologies *The Best of Chess Life & Review,* Volumes I and II, and has produced, with David MacEnuity, two instructional videotapes, *Understanding Chess* and *Opening Principles.*

Bruce was the chief commentator at the New York half of the 1990 Kasparov-Karpov World Chess Championship, and in 1990 was head coach of the United States Team in the World Youth Chess Championships in Wisconsin. Perhaps the most experienced chess teacher in North America, he is co-founder, with Faneuil Adams, of the Manhattan Chess Club School and is the director of the New York City Schools Program. Bruce's most famous student, six-time national Scholastic Champion Joshua Waitzkin, is the subject of Fred Waitzkin's acclaimed book *Searching for Bobby Fischer* and of the movie of the same name. Bruce Pandolfini lives in New York City.